# Thirty-two *Cantigas d'amigo* of Dom Dinis: Typology of a Portuguese Renunciation

by

Rip Cohen

Madison, 1987

Created through the generous patronage of the
Division of Research Programs
of the

# National Endowment for the Humanities

Portuguese Series, No. 1

Copyright ©1987 by
The Hispanic Seminary of
Medieval Studies, Ltd.

ISBN 0-94-2260-55-4

to
Keith Aldrich
and
Jorge de Sena

qui solebant
meas esse aliquid putare nugas

# Acknowledgements

I am grateful to the Fundação Calouste Gulbenkian, of Lisbon, for two grants which allowed me time to study and, eventually, to formulate this thesis. This work would never have come into being had it not been for Keith Aldrich, Jorge de Sena, Mécia de Sena, Donald Pearce, Alva Walter Bennett, Maria de Lourdes Belchior, and Luciana Stegagno Picchio. To them all—would I could thank them all—my deepest gratitude. I would also like to thank Professor Harvey Sharrer, who offered advice and encouragement, and Dra. Elsa Gonçalves, who was kind enough to read *cantigas* with me while I was in Lisbon. In addition many people have helped me at different times in my studies and travels, both scholars and friends, and some who are both. To these people, and above all to my friends, I offer gratitude in silence, "least the world should taske you to recite / what merit liv'd in me . . ."

# Table of Contents

Introduction . . . . . . . . . . . . . . . . . . . . . . . . . . . . . . . . . . i
Chapter One: Komos and Renunciation: The Male Discourse . . . . . . . 1
    The Komos in the *Cantiga*: A *Schema* . . . . . . . . . . . . . . . 1
    "Senhor fremosa, vejo-vos queixar" . . . . . . . . . . . . . . . . 3
    "Oi mais quer'eu ja leixá-lo trobar" . . . . . . . . . . . . . . 7
Chapter Two: The Thirty-two *Cantigas* . . . . . . . . . . . . . . . . 13
    Naming Things . . . . . . . . . . . . . . . . . . . . . . . . 13
    Criteria . . . . . . . . . . . . . . . . . . . . . . . . . . . 14
    Texts and Analysis . . . . . . . . . . . . . . . . . . . . . . 18
      1. "bẽ entendi meu amigo" . . . . . . . . . . . . . . . . 19
      2. "amiga muyt a grã sazõ" . . . . . . . . . . . . . . . 21
      3. "que trist oi e meu amigo" . . . . . . . . . . . . . . 23
      4. "dos que ora son na oste" . . . . . . . . . . . . . . 25
    Summary of *cantigas* 1-4 . . . . . . . . . . . . . . . . . . 27
      5. "que muyt a ia que nõ veio" . . . . . . . . . . . . . 27
      6. "chegou m or aqui recado" . . . . . . . . . . . . . . 29
      7. "o meu amig amiga nõ quer eu" . . . . . . . . . . . . 32
      8. "amiga bõ grad aia deus" . . . . . . . . . . . . . . 34
    Summary of *cantigas* 1-8 . . . . . . . . . . . . . . . . . . 35
      9. "vos que vos en vossos cantares meu" . . . . . . . . . 36
     10. "roga m oie filha o voss amig[o]" . . . . . . . . . . 38
     11. "pesar mi fez meu amigo" . . . . . . . . . . . . . . 39
     12. "amiga ssey eu bẽ dunha molher" . . . . . . . . . . . 41
    Summary of *cantigas* 1-12 . . . . . . . . . . . . . . . . . 42
     13. "bon dya vi amigo" . . . . . . . . . . . . . . . . . 43
     14. "non chegou madre o meu amigo" . . . . . . . . . . . 45
     15. "de que moiredes filha a do corpo velido" . . . . . . 47
     16. "ay flores ay flores do verde pyno" . . . . . . . . . 50
    Summary of *cantigas* 1-16 . . . . . . . . . . . . . . . . . 52
     17. "levantou ss a velida" . . . . . . . . . . . . . . . 55
     18. "amigu e meu amigo" . . . . . . . . . . . . . . . . . 57
     19. "o voss amigo tã de coraçõ" . . . . . . . . . . . . . 59
     20. "c[o]m ousara parecer ante mi" . . . . . . . . . . . 61
     21. "en grave dia senhor que vos oy" . . . . . . . . . . 63
     22. "amiga faço me maravilhada" . . . . . . . . . . . . . 64
     23. "o voss amig amiga vi andar" . . . . . . . . . . . . 67
     24. "amigo queredes vos hir" . . . . . . . . . . . . . . 68
     25. "dizede por [d]eus amigo" . . . . . . . . . . . . . . 70
     26. "non poss eu meu amigo" . . . . . . . . . . . . . . . 72

27. "por deus amigo quẽ cuydaria" . . . . . . . . . . . . . . . . 75
28. "o meu amigo a de mal assaz" . . . . . . . . . . . . . . . 76
29. "meu amigo nõ poss eu guarecer" . . . . . . . . . . . . 78
30. "que coyta ouvestes madr e senhor" . . . . . . . . . 80
31. "amigu e falss e desleal" . . . . . . . . . . . . . . . . . . 82
32. "meu amigo ven oi aqui" . . . . . . . . . . . . . . . . . 85
Chapter Three: Findings . . . . . . . . . . . . . . . . . . . . . . 87
    Personae . . . . . . . . . . . . . . . . . . . . . . . . . . . 87
    The Sequence of Genres . . . . . . . . . . . . . . . . . 91
    The Affective Disposition of the Girl . . . . . . . . . . . 92
    Symmetries . . . . . . . . . . . . . . . . . . . . . . . . 93
    Fiinda . . . . . . . . . . . . . . . . . . . . . . . . . . . 97
Notes . . . . . . . . . . . . . . . . . . . . . . . . . . . . . . . . 101
Appendices . . . . . . . . . . . . . . . . . . . . . . . . . . . . 121
    1. The Breakdown of Six Komoi . . . . . . . . . . . . . . 121
    2. Rhymes in Poem-Final Position . . . . . . . . . . . . 130
Bibliography . . . . . . . . . . . . . . . . . . . . . . . . . . . . 133

# Introduction

One of the most interesting theoretical problems concerning medieval poetry is that of the so called theory of genres.[1] It seems obvious enough that there can be no categorization or classification of materials until those materials have been adequately described.[2] In the case of medieval Galego-Portuguese love lyric, there has not yet been a systematic description of the types of discourse found in the corpus.

Giuseppe Tavani, in his essay "La poesia lirica galego-portoghese," has tried to give an objective description of the three "genres"—*cantigas d'amor, cantigas d'amigo*, and *cantigas d'escarnh'e de maldizer*—into which the corpus has traditionally been divided.[3] Of these, only two, the *cantigas d'amor* and *cantigas d'amigo*, concern us here, since the third lies beyond the bounds of what is commonly called love poetry.[4] The traditional distinction between *cantigas d'amor* and *cantigas d'amigo* is based largely on the criterion offered at the very beginning of the fragmentary, untitled, anonymous *poetica* in Cod. 10991 of the *Biblioteca Nacional*, Lisbon.[5]

> e por que algũas cantigas hy ha en que falam eles e elas outrossy, por ẽ he bem de entenderdes se som d'amor, se d'amigo, por que sabede que, se eles falam na prima cobra e elas na outra, amor, por que se move a rrazõ d'ele, como vos ante dissemos; e se elas falam na primeira cobra, he outrossy d'amigo; e se ambos falam ẽ hũa cobra, outrossy he segundo qual d'eles fala na cobra primeiro.[6]

But this criterion, though reflected in the organization of the manuscripts, is not always valid, and is far from being—nor does it pretend to be—an adequate description of the two genres.[7] Tavani's description of the *cantiga d'amor* is accurate in its main points, although he seems not to have taken sufficient notice of the existence of a genre which has been called the Renunciation, and whose structure I have outlined elsewhere.[8] The four principal semic fields ("campi semici") which Tavani ascribes to the *cantiga d'amor* correspond exactly to topoi of the male wooing speech, or, as it has been called, the *Komos*: 1) the speaker's love and love-service; 2) praise of the beloved; 3) the beloved's "cruelty;" and 4) the speaker's amorous suffering.[9] The most basic topos of the Komos is the "request for amorous favors," and as Tavani observes, the *cantiga d'amor* is nearly always structured as a request for amorous favors.[10] He does not, however, cede the topos of request status as a semic field. Nor, of course, does he grant such status to a type of discourse (the Renunciation) distinct from such requests. But it should be noted that, even in Tavani's analysis, the wooing speech in medieval Galego-Portuguese love lyric may be identified by the personae involved (a male lover and a female beloved) and by the situation existing between them, which (it must be conceded) is nearly always a situation of courtship. For when he comes to describe the *cantiga d'amigo*, Tavani insists that it can be analyzed as an articulation of five semic fields. Yet the fact is that the *cantiga d'amor*, in so far as it can be considered synonymous with the Komos, represents a single type of situation, a single type of discourse, whereas the *cantiga d'amigo* is characterized precisely by a diversity of situations and discourses.[11] Thus it might be more accurate to say that the *cantiga d'amigo* is not a genre, but the location of a complex of genres.[12]

I wish to reject most of the standard definitions of "genre," but I cannot ground my discourse outside of time and history. I begin, therefore, by going backwards, because poetics directs us to look at a text as a synchronic structure which fits into a frame in a diachronic dialectic of forms and practices. In certain fundamental respects, poetic genre has been well treated by Francis Cairns, in *Generic Composition in Greek and Roman Poetry*, 1972, who finds that genre is defined by primary and secondary elements. The primary elements are the speaker, the addressee, and the situation. The secondary elements, which Cairns calls *topoi*, are the smallest thematic elements useful for generic analysis. (Topoi, in this sense are not the *loci communes* of Curtius et al.) Each genre makes use of a set of topoi, but any topos may be common to more than one genre, so that the "only final arbiters of generic identity," says Cairns, must be the primary elements.[13] The actual speaker need not be the logical speaker—in the *cantigas*, for instance, a friend may deliver a wooing speech to the girl on behalf of the boy—and the actual addressee need not be the logical addressee (e.g., the girl may address her female friend in discourses which are logically directed to the boy).[14]

In this thesis, a topos will not be considered as part of the utterance. That is to say, a topos is not uttered, but is referred to. What is uttered might better be called a thematic unit, or, its smallest form (a single lexeme, such as "cruel!"), a minimal thematic unit. The thematic unit refers to the topos in the same way that text refers to its genre. The relation between topos and genre is purely logical. The statement, "you are cruel," bears a logical relation to the topical request, "please be kind to me." This logical relation is not syntagmatically articulated in the relation between topos and genre, however; the syntagmatic articulation of the relation between the two "ideas" belongs to the text, the utterance, in which grammatical syntax supplies the link. Syntagmatic interrelation of thematic units is important to my understanding of generic structure, as that structure is found articulated in the text. "Syntagmatic interrelation of thematic units" is admittedly awkward. I would, therefore, replace it with the simpler "sequence of functions." This phrase, as I shall use it here, will be understood to mean the sequence of thematic units as they are actualized in the utterance which is the text. Sequence of functions in a text can be taken as equivalent to text as signifier (text signifies sequence of functions) and to genre as signified (the sequence of functions signifies the genre).

The corpus of the love poetry of Dom Dinis which has been transmitted to us consists of 128 texts, divided in the manuscripts as follows:[15]

1. 75 *cantigas d'amor*

2. 52 *cantigas d'amigo*
3. 1 *cantiga d'amor*[16]

The corpus which I am presenting consists of the first 32 *cantigas d'amigo* found in the manuscripts. They appear in the same order in both manuscripts and are followed in both by a *cantiga d'amigo* in which the persona is a married woman, the only persona who can be so identified in the corpus of Dom Dinis.[17] The 32 texts are thus set off at both ends—at the beginning, by being the first *cantigas d'amigo*, and by a rubric in the manuscripts which so defines them, and at the end by a text which clearly does not belong in the sequence.[18]

The actual speaker and addressee can be identified in each of the 32 *cantigas* in this corpus by textual evidence or by textually supportable inferences, except in the case of nos. 16 and 17. In the former the speaker of the verses (not the *refram*) in stanzas 5-8 is unidentified. In no. 17 the persona of the speaker of the entire text is indeterminate. The speakers in the remaining texts of the corpus of 32 *cantigas* are identified in the chart on pp. 87-88. They are: the girl, the girl's mother, the girl's female friend, the boy.[19] There is nothing within the corpus which would enable us to distinguish the girl, the mother, the friend, or the boy in one text from his or her counterpart in any of the other texts in the set. These four personae, along with the unidentified voice(s), are used by the poet in, apparently, a carefully organized way.

The boy, for instance, does not appear in the first half. He speaks in dialogs with the girl in the sixth and seventh groups of four (nos. 21-28). His first appearance as speaker—in the text in first position in the sixth group of four—corresponds exactly to the first appearance of his message—in the sixth text in the first group of eight. In the first half, he is addressee (present or absent he is the logical addressee) only in texts in the first position in their respective groups of four; in the second half, the two dialogs in which he and the girl have an equal division of verses also come in the first position in the respective groups of four. The text in which he dominates (20 verses to the girl's 4) is no. 24, which marks the end of the third group of eight (3/4 point in the series). This is one of the climactic moments in the drama: having sent various messages, appeared in person and been rebuffed, the boy threatens to go off into exile, and the girl begins to relent. The mother appears only in the third and fourth groups of four in each half, and only once outside the fourth group. The friend fades out in the second quarter and again in the last (i.e., in the second and fourth groups of eight) and is not present in the last group of four in either half. The unidentified voices are heard only in the two texts on either side of the center of the series.

This seemingly systematic distribution of the primary elements of speaker and addressee is more than evidence of the poet's intention to write a series; it is a formal technique by which the lyric drama is articulated. It should be noted that in the seventy-six *cantigas d'amor* of Dom Dinis the male persona is the only speaker in seventy-three of the texts, and that in the remaining twenty *cantigas d'amigo* the girl speaks in eighteen, a friend in two.[20] Thus the proportion of texts in which someone other than the principal persona speaks is as follows with respect to these three sections of the corpus of love poetry by Dom Dinis:

1. 76 *cantigas d'amor*:     3/76
2. 32 *cantigas d'amigo*:   13/32
3. 20 *cantigas d'amigo*:   2/20

These proportions show clearly that our corpus of 32 *cantigas d'amigo* has, in the purely formal elements of speaker and addressee variation, a dramatic potential which neither of the other groups possesses. This potential is actualized by the sequence of genres in the series.

These 32 *cantigas* form a macro-poem which is structured as the image of a *cantiga*. Structural components in this macro-text differ from those in an individual *cantiga*, to be sure, but it would not be inaccurate to say that within the macro-poem the individual *cantiga* is roughly equivalent to a verse-unit, and that the "strophes" are of eight *cantigas* each—thus a macro-poem of four strophes, with eight verses to the strophe.

In its massive strophic alignments, and in its sequence of genres, the macro-poem reflects the conceptual structures of the *cantiga*. Thus the distribution, within a *cantiga*, of thematic elements in positions which are symmetrical with respect to the strophic structure of the *cantiga* (what is commonly called "parallelism") is reflected within the macro-poem by the distribution of genres in positions which are symmetrical with respect to the strophic construction of the macro-poem.

In regard to the distribution both of functions within a *cantiga* and of genres within the macro-poem, we would do well to look at the description in the *ars poetica* (in B) of the *fiinda*.[21]

as fiindas som cousa que os trobadores sempre husaron de poer en acabamento das sas cantigas pera cõncludirẽ e acabaren melhor en elas as rrazones que disserõ nas cantigas chamandolhis fiinda por que quer tanto dizer come acabamẽto de rrazõ.[22]

The word "rrazõ", which figures both here and in the section of the *poetica* cited above, must clearly mean several things. First of all, it is equivalent to "speech." Secondly, it means "discourse" in the precise sense of "course of the utterance." Thirdly, and above all, it must mean "logic," in the sense of "logical development." The *cantiga* is a form, and the "rrazones" are contained within the *cantiga*.` The *fiinda* is a place in the *cantiga*, and within it the "rrazõ" is concluded and completed. The relation between the form of the poem and a place within that form, the *fiinda*, as well as the relation between the form of the poem and the discourse within it, and, in addition, the relation between the body of the discourse and its logical conclusion (in the *fiinda*) are all expressed in this simple phrase. Implied also is the understanding that the shape of the discourse (not the shape of the *cantiga*, but of the "rrazõ") is contained within the *cantiga*, and, in turn, contains within itself the "substance" of the "rrazõ", that is, the specific utterance of a specific text.

After saying, with what seems nearly a philosophic precision, that the *fiinda* is the location of the logical conclusion of the "rrazõ" the *poetica* reverses itself and says that the *fiinda* is equivalent—not to the end of the *cantiga*—but to the ending of the "rrazõ" ("acabamẽto de rrazõ").

In this study I shall regard the *fiinda* as part of the musical form, and call the conclusion of the "rrazõ" the "cadential function," with the understanding that cadential functions are not found only in *fiindas*, but in *refrans*, and generally at the end of each stanza and of each poem. Any cadential function signals the direction of the sequence of functions at that point in the sequence whether or not the sequence is concluded. Thus a *refram* in an initial stanza (within a *cantiga* of more than one stanza) may conclude the sequence of functions in the first stanza, but the *fiinda* (or, lacking one, the last verse) of the same text will be the index of the direction of the sequence at the "final cadence," or end of the poem. A cadential function is the clearest sign of the generic identity of the sequence which it concludes.

The cadential function also will have its counterpart in the macro-poem. Just as, within the structuration of the individual *cantiga*, the end of each stanza and the end of the poem are privileged positions (both musically and thematically), so the end of each "strophe" in the macro-poem (that is, the last *cantiga* in each "strophe:" nos. 8, 16, 24, 32) will be privileged *a priori* by the underlying form, both musical and thematic, of the macro-poem. In other words, just as the individual *cantiga* is delimited by the mathematical proportions and symmetries of its formal components (verses and strophes) and designated from within by the direction of its sequence of functions, so the macro-poem is delimited in its physical extension by the precise mathematical proportion and symmetries of its "verses" (*cantigas*) and "strophes" (groups of eight *cantigas*), and designated from within by the direction of its sequence of genres. Since—*quod demonstrandum est*—it designates its own direction as renunciatory, I shall be arguing that this macro-poem represents the history of a renunciation. It is in this sense that a description and analysis of the sequence of discourse-types by which this history is articulated might be called the typology of a renunciation.[23]

# Chapter One

## i

## The Komos in the *Cantiga*: A *Schema*

In the typology of the *cantigas d'amigo* the male Komos figures as a genre, sometimes with a substitute (female) speaker, other times spoken by a male persona in person. It will be convenient, therefore, to look briefly at the structure of the Komos in the *cantiga d'amor*.

The four "campi semici" which, according to Tavani, characterize "tipologicamente" the *cantiga d'amor*, are "elogio della dama," "amore del poeta per lei," "riserbo della dama," and "pena per un amore non corrisposto."[1] Adding to these the topos of "request" (which, as I have mentioned, does not figure among the "campi semici" of Tavani) we may, for the sake of convenience, refer to the five main topoi of the male Komos as: 1) Service; 2) Praise; 3) Suffering; 4) Cruelty; 5) Request.

To see how this sequence of functions is articulated in the love poetry of Dom Dinis we could look at nearly any of his *cantigas d'amor*, but perhaps the most revealing view of this type of sequence is to be found in an "included" example of the genre—a brief Komos quoted by a female speaker in one of the *cantigas d'amigo* of Dom Dinis which is not in our corpus of thirty-two: "Falou-m' oj' o meu amigo" (Lang CXXVI). This type of phenomenon, an example of a genre included within an example of the same or another genre, is referred to by F. Cairns as an included generic example.[2]

In that *cantiga d'amigo*, the female speaker (whom I shall call "the girl"), addressing a female friend (whom I shall call "the friend"), tells how her male friend (whom I shall call "the boy") humbly spoke with her, pleading his love, and was sent away without a consoling response. Thereupon the girl quotes what she says the boy told her. This passage is of interest not only for the concision with which it phrases the topoi of the Komos, but because, constituting, as it does, an "included" example of the genre, it is a perfect example of a male komos in a *cantiga d'amor*.

> Disse-m' el: Senhor, creede
> que a vossa fremosura
> mi faz gram mal sem mesura,
> porem de mi vos doede.[3]

What the girl tells her friend that the boy told her is that she should believe that her beauty causes him great harm ("bad" is his word), and should therefore feel sorry for him. The sequence of functions here can be identified by specific lexical items, thus: "senhor" implies service; "vossa fermosura", praise; "gram mal", suffering; "sem mesura", cruelty; and "vos doede", the request. If, then, we designate these five topoi, in the order in which they appear in this included Komos, by the Greek letters "$\alpha$" (=service), "$\beta$" (=praise), "$\gamma$" (=suffering), "$\delta$" (=cruelty), "$\epsilon$" (=request), we can say that the sequence of functions is precisely $\alpha>\beta>\gamma>\delta>\epsilon$. These functions may occur in any sequence within a Komos, and any one of these functions can be cadential within a komastic sequence. The following *schema* (in which the poems are referred to by the number in V, the manuscript on which Lang's text is based) shows the sequence of functions in each of six *cantigas d'amor* of Dom Dinis (which are broken down into topoi in Appendix 1):

V 100:

| | | | | | |
|---|---|---|---|---|---|
| I | $\gamma$ | $\epsilon$ | | | |
| II | $\delta$ | $\gamma$ | $\epsilon$ | | |
| III | $\delta$ | $\gamma$ | $\epsilon$ | | |
| IV | $\delta$ | $\gamma$ | $\epsilon$ | | |

V 125

| | | | | | |
|---|---|---|---|---|---|
| I | $\gamma$ | $\beta$ | $\gamma$ | $\alpha$ | |
| II | $\beta$ | $\gamma$ | $\alpha$ | | |
| III | $\epsilon$ | $\gamma$ | $\delta$ | $\gamma$ | $\alpha$ |

V 141

| | | | |
|---|---|---|---|
| I | $\alpha$ | $\epsilon$ | $\gamma$ |
| II | $\gamma$ | $\epsilon$ | $\gamma$ |
| III | $\gamma$ | $\epsilon$ | $\gamma$ |

V 149

| | | | | | |
|---|---|---|---|---|---|
| I | $\epsilon$ | $\alpha$ | $\delta$ | $\gamma$ | $\epsilon$ | $\delta$ |
| II | $\epsilon$ | $\alpha$ | $\delta$ | $\gamma$ | $\epsilon$ | $\delta$ |
| III | $\epsilon$ | $\alpha$ | $\delta$ | $\gamma$ | $\epsilon$ | $\delta$ |
| IV | $\epsilon$ | $\beta$ | $\alpha$ | $\epsilon$ | $\beta$ | $\delta$ |
| V | $\epsilon$ | | | | | |

V 153

| I | γ | β | ε | β |
|---|---|---|---|---|
| II | β | ε | β | |
| III | ε | γ | ε | β |

V 155

| I | γ | δ | β | ε | γ |
|---|---|---|---|---|---|
| II | β | α | ε | γ | |
| III | γ | β | ε | γ | |
| IV | α | | | | |

α: service
β: praise
γ: suffering
δ: cruelty
ε: request

These six poems (translations of which are also given in Appendix 1) are not, of course, reducible to a succesion of letters, but the sequence of functions in each of them can be represented in this simple way, and the classification of this kind of poem as a genre is based on the existence of a large group of poems (more than 60 among the *cantigas d'amor* of Dom Dinis alone) whose sequences of functions conform to this type.

To demonstrate the existence of another genre among the *cantigas d'amor* of Dom Dinis, it will suffice, therefore, to analyze two texts, "Senhor fremosa, vejo-vos queixar," (Lang LXVI) and "Oi mais quer' eu ja leixá-lo trobar" (Lang II), in each of which the sequence of functions is not of the type analyzed in the schema above.

ii

| I | 1. | Senhor fremosa, vejo-vos queixar |
|---|----|-----------------------------------|
| | 2. | por que vos am', e no meu coraçom |
| | 3. | ei mui gram pesar, se Deus mi perdom, |

|      |    |                                      |
|------|----|--------------------------------------|
|      | 4. | porque vej' end' a vós aver pesar,   |
|      | 5. | e queria-m'em de grado quitar,       |
|      | 6. | mais nom posso forçar o coraçom,     |

|     |    |                                        |
|-----|----|----------------------------------------|
| II  | 1. | Que mi forçou meu saber e meu sem;     |
|     | 2. | desi meteu-me no vosso poder,          |
|     | 3. | e do pesar que vos eu vej' aver,       |
|     | 4. | par Deus, senhor, a mim pesa muit' em; |
|     | 5. | e partir-m' ia de vós querer bem,      |
|     | 6. | mais tolhe-m' end' o coraçom poder,    |

|     |    |                                      |
|-----|----|--------------------------------------|
| III | 1. | Que me forçou de tal guisa, senhor,  |
|     | 2. | que sem nem força nom ei ja de mi;   |
|     | 3. | e do pesar que vós tomades i,        |
|     | 4. | tom' eu pesar que nom posso maior,   |
|     | 5. | e queria nom vos aver amor,          |
|     | 6. | mais o coraçom póde mais ca mi.      |

Lovely lady, I see you complain
that I love you, and in my heart
I have very great pain, so help me God,
since I see that you have pain from that,
and I would gladly get myself out of this,
but I cannot force the heart

Which has forced my mind and my sense
since it put me in your power,
and from the pain that I see you have,
by God, Lady, I have much pain,
and I would like to stop wanting you,
but my heart takes away the power

For it has forced me to such an extent, Lady,
that I have no sense or control of myself any more,
and from the pain that you feel from that
I feel such pain that I cannot feel more,
and I would love not to love you,
but the heart has more power than me.

This text begins with what appears to be a Komastic sequence: 1) praise ("senhor fremosa" I 1); 2) cruelty ("vejo-vos queixar / porque vos am'" I 1-2); 3) service ("porque vos am'" I 2); 4) suffering ("e no meu coraçom / ei mui gram pesar" I 2-3). The speaker suffers because the Lady is pained by his love of her: porque vej' end a vós aver pesar (I 4).

The provisional conclusion to this sequence is not the request which caps all the Komoi mentioned above, but a function which does not appear in any of them, that of the desire to renounce:

(I 5)      e queria-m'em de grado quitar."

This desire is expressed by a verb in the imperfect indicative, corresponding here to the conditional: "I would gladly extract myself from this (situation)." But the conditional mood ("queria") is contrasted with the indicatives ("nom posso," "forçou," "meteu"):

(I 6)      mais nom posso forçar o coraçom

(II 1)      Que mi forcou meu saber e meu sem;
(II 2)      desi meteu-me no vosso poder

At this point the circular (or spiralling) logical structure begins to repeat itself. Some form of the word "pesar" occurs in the third and fourth lines of each stanza, once with reference to the pain the lady feels because of the speaker's love, and once with reference to the pain he feels knowing that she feels pain. The fifth line of each stanza expresses the speaker's desire to renounce, but the impossibility of realizing this desire is the subject of the sixth line of each stanza, and this subject is continued in the first two lines of stanzas two and three by means of a relative pronoun, "que", referring to the "coraçom" mentioned in the last line of the preceding stanza. Thus,

(I 5)      e queria-m' em de grado quitar,
(1 6)      mais nom posso forçar o coraçom,

(II 1)      Que mi forçou meu saber e meu sem;

. . .

(II 5)      e partir-m' ia de vós querer bem
(II 6)      mais tolhe-m' end' o coraçom poder

(III 1)      Que me forçou . . .

(III 5)      e queria nom vos aver amor,
(III 6)      mais o coraçom póde mais ca mi.

It could be argued that the speaker's desire to renounce his lady is part of his love service, since it is to spare her pain that he wants to stop loving her.[4] Similarly, it could be argued that his inability to renounce is proof-of-love, and that the whole text is enkomiastic since it is her power over him that precludes renunciation.[5] As for the first argument, it may be observed that his assertion that he suffers pain at seeing her pain may very well be an ironic statement of intense frustration: "Believe me, when I see how my love of you upsets you, I too am upset." To the second objection it may be said that it is his heart and not her beauty that is responsible for thwarting his renunciatory intent. His heart has overpowered both his knowledge and his judgment (II 1), and left him neither sense nor power over himself. This realization of his folly may be assigned to the "present clarity" topos.[6] The speaker seems to be criticizing his inability to extract himself from a hopeless situation.

Perhaps the most obvious signal that the poem is a Renunciation is the repeated articulation of the desire to renounce, in the fifth line of each stanza. The desire to renounce displaces the request as the conclusion of the sequential logic. Even if renunciation is impossible (and it is this assertion which has, in the merry-go-round of the text, the "final" say), it is renunciation which the speaker says he desires. That is his project.

Moreover, the statement of the desire to renounce is rhythmically privileged by the fact that the verses in which it occurs—the fifth (penultimate) line of each stanza—are the only verses in the text in which: 1) there is no word accent in either of the first two syllables; and 2) the third syllable, accented, contains a long "i." This crypto-parallelism in the fifth verse of each stanza also helps to elucidate the meaning of the phrases used here to express the desire to renounce.

(I 5)        e queria-m' em de grado quitar

(II 5)       e partir-m'ia de vós querer bem

(III 5)      e queria nom vos aver amor

The meaning of "m'em ... quitar" is clarified by "partir ... de vós querer bem" and finally by "nom vos aver amor," so that the act of leaving is seen to be equivalent to the renunciation of love, at least to the attempt to renounce.

The gradual intensification in the expression of the pain the speaker feels corresponds to the increasing clarity with which he articulates his desire to renounce:

(I 3)        ei mui gram pesar

(II 4)       a mim pesa muit'em

(III 4)      tom'eu pesar que nom posso maior

Thus the strongest expression of his pain (III 4) is followed by the strongest expression of his desire to stop loving:

| (III 4) | tom'eu pesar que nom posso maior |
|---|---|
| (III 5) | e queria nom vos aver amor |

which suggests that the topical logic is: 1) suffering; 2) desire to renounce. It is the speaker's pain, not his devotion to the lady, which prompts him to want to leave ("partir"), to stop loving ("nom . . . aver amor").

The speaker cannot force his heart (I 6, II 6, III 6), since he has lost his rational power (II 1-2; III 1-2), and although his desire to renounce increases even during the course of the text, he knows that such a renunciation is impossible. However impossible the renunciation, the sequence of functions in such a text is easily distinguished from the sequences found in the six Komoi.


## iii


I       1.    Oi mais quer' eu ja leixá-lo trobar
              2.    e quero-me desemparar d'amor,
              3.    e quer' ir algunha terra buscar
              4.    u nunca possa seer sabedor
              5.    ela de mi nem eu de mha senhor,
              6.    pois que lh' e d'eu viver aqui pesar.

II      1.    Mais Deus! que grave cousa d'endurar
              2.    que a mim será ir-me d'u ela fôr;
              3.    ca sei mui bem que nunca poss' achar
              4.    nenhũa cousa ond' aja sabor,
              5.    se nom da morte; mais ar ei pavor
              6.    de mh a nom querer Deus tam cedo dar.

III     1.    Mais se fez Deus a tam gram coita par
              2.    come a de que serei sofredor,
              3.    quando m'agora ouver d'alongar
              4.    d'aquesta terra u est a melhor
              5.    de quantas som, e de cujo loor

6.     nom se póde per dizer acabar.


From now on I want to stop singing,
and I want to free myself from love,
and I want to go find some land
where it will never be possible
for my lady to know about me, or me about her,
since for her my living here is pain.

But God, what a crushing thing to endure
that I should go away from where she were,
for I know very well that I could never find
anything of which I might have savor,
except death; but now I am afraid
that God won't want to give me it so quickly.

I doubt God made himself so great a pain
as that of which I shall be sufferer
when I shall have to go away
from this land where is the best
of all that are, and whose praise
it is not possible to stop singing.


The desire to renounce is clearly expressed at the beginning of this *cantiga*.[7]
Curiously, though the text contains three stanzas of six lines each, the only clauses
which can with certainty be identified as main clauses are the three which open the
poem and which express the desire to renounce.

(I 1-3)     Oi mais quer' eu ja leixá-lo trobar
            e quero-me desemparar d'amor,
            e quer' ir algunha terra buscar

The present situation is defined in a series of three statements, each expressing
a desire, each introduced by the word "quer(o)." But the desire expressed by the
speaker is not the usual desire to win the love of the lady. The desire is: 1) to stop
singing; 2) to flee from love; 3) to go into exile. "Not to sing" is to renounce. Thus
the desire to stop singing is equivalent to the desire to renounce. This identification is
immediately confirmed in the second line, which contains an explicit, non-figurative
formulation of the desire to renounce. The third line introduces a third clause,

extending through the rest of the stanza, and containing yet another formulation of the desire to renounce: "and I want to go look for some land." The land he desires to find would have to be one "u nunca possa seer sabedor / ela de mi nem eu de mha senhor." It must be a land where no information can filter through either to the speaker or to his lady concerning the other. Thus the function of this land will be to isolate the speaker. The land of exile is a metaphor for the "world" of renunciation, into which, ideally, no signs of the beloved could enter.[8]

The reason for the speaker's triple wish is given in I 6: "pois que lh' e d'eu viver aqui pesar." He wishes to renounce because his "living here" bothers his lady. This reason for renouncing, which corresponds to the classical "unwillingness of the beloved," casts a new light on the desire to renounce, since it is ambiguous, precisely as it was in "Senhor fremosa, vejo vos queixar." It is not clear whether 1) he wants to renounce because she is so "cruel"; or 2) he wants not to incommode her. In the first case, the renunciation would be an attempt to save himself, and possibly even a form of vengeance.[9] In the second case the renunciation would be an extreme example of the "service" topos of the Komos, and would constitute proof of his love.

The speaker's stance softens in the second stanza:

> (II 1-6)  Mais Deus! que grave cousa d'endurar
> que a mim será ir-me d'u ela fôr;
> ca sei mui bem que nunca poss' achar
> nenhũa cousa ond' aja sabor,
> se nom da morte; mais ar ei pavor
> de mh a nom querer Deus tam cedo dar.

This exclamation responds specifically to the desires stated in the first stanza. He would like to go, but it would be a "grave cousa" to leave the place where she is (II 1-2). He will thereafter have no pleasure (II 3-4) except death (II 5), but is afraid that God will not grant it to him quickly enough (II 5-6).

Among the *cantigas d'amor* of Dom Dinis, it is ordinarily in the Komos that the speaker says that he can find no pleasure in anything but a speedy death if the lady does not have mercy. Such declarations in Komoi belong to the "suffering" topos. The desire for death is thus often a measure of the speaker's suffering, and not, as in "Quant' eu, fremosa mha senhor" (Lang V), a desire to renounce by the only available means: termination of life. But since the desire for death is a polyvalent topos, which could have two different generic implications, its use here at the end of the second stanza prolongs the generic ambiguity of the text.

The third stanza begins with an exclamation:

> (III 1-4)  Mais se fez Deus a tam gram coita par
> come a de que serei sofredor,
> quando m'agora ouver d'alongar
> d'aquesta terra

The generic analysis of this section is problematical. In the context of what is apparently a Renunciation it would seem to belong to the topos "inability to renounce" or "conflict." But what follows is specifically enkomiastic, i.e., belonging to the (komastic) topos "praise of the beloved":

> (III 4-6)          . . . u est a melhor
> de quantas som, e de cujo loor
> nom se póde per dizer acabar

The finale would seem, retroactively, to color the opening of the stanza, which thus could be considered to belong to the komastic topos, "suffering." Yet the speaker continues to refer to his imminent exile ("quando m'agora ouver d'alongar / d'aquesta terra" III 3-4).

The assignment of the generic material of III 1-2 depends then, on the overall generic context, which is itself ambiguous. It should be noted that the material in the text which would belong to the topos of "conflict," if the poem were a renunciation, would belong to the topos of "suffering," were it a Komos. The poem seems to develop simultaneously along parallel lines and to invoke the matrices of both Komos and Renunciation. The resulting polyvalent sequence can be schematized as follows:

| I   | 1-5 |          |     | Renunciation |     |
| --- | --- | -------- | --- | ------------ | --- |
| I   | 6   | Cruelty  | (R) | Service      | (K) |
| II  | 1-6 | Conflict | (R) | Suffering    | (K) |
| III | 1-4 | Conflict | (R) | Suffering    | (K) |
| III | 4-6 | Conflict | (R) | Praise       | (K) |

The poem opens with three clear statements of the desire to renounce: "quer' ... quero ... quer' ..." The exclamation "Mais Deus!, que grave cousa" (II 1), which responds to these, leads off into a possible modulation. For the purposes of this analysis we can consider that the generic material (topoi) of each genre constitutes a *harmonic sphere*.[10] An ambiguous topos is one which, capable of functioning within either harmonic sphere, can be used either to effect a modulation from one sphere (genre) to the other or to suggest such a modulation, without actualizing it. Viewed within the context of a Renunciation, the second stanza represents the conflict which the speaker feels at the prospect of exile. We could, without analyzing details, represent this sequence as "renunciation" > "conflict", and expect the next section to mark a continuation of the Renunciation, that is "renunciation" > "conflict" > "renunciation". But if the sequence were "renunciation" > "suffering" > "komos", the center section would prove to have been a modulation to the harmonic sphere of the Komos.

If such a modulation does not take place, if the Renunciation is reasserted, the central section could be considered a potential but not actualized modulation, a *pivot chord* which pivots back to the first genre instead of into the second, which it only momentarily evokes. In this text the modulation does seem to take place, finally, in the last verse and a half of the poem ("e de cujo loor / nom se póde per dizer acabar") and the sequence would thus appear to be: "renunciation" > "suffering" > "praise" (K). But though the final function—which we shall call, in keeping with the musical terminology, the *cadential* function—is komastic, this fact does not allow us to resolve the question of generic identity as easily as might seem. Renunciations often have a cadential function drawn from the harmonic sphere of the Komos. Yet this type of sequence, which we may designate R(1,2,3...)k is a renunciatory sequence.

An elaborate form of this kind of sequence is found in Ovid, *Amores* 3.11, studied by Cairns.[11] Scholars had for a long time divided that poem, considering it two separate texts, precisely because they did not understand that Renunciations traditionally contain what Cairns calls a "reaction."[12] Within the duration of the text the would-be renouncer often reacts and changes his mind. Thus the sequence R(1,2,3,...)k appears in Ovid *Amores* 3.11 as R(1,2,3...) > K(1,2,3...). In sequences of the first type the abbreviated Komos, which can be represented by any of its topoi, appears as a function within a renunciatory sequence. The second case can be analyzed in two ways: 1) the komastic function is expanded so as to constitute an "included example" of the genre Komos; 2) the poem belongs to a third, compound genre, which can be designated as R > K.

It is not clear which of these structures "Oi mais quer' eu ja leixá-lo trobar" represents, and the generic assignment will depend on where the komastic reaction is thought to begin. Since the second stanza and most of the third contain ambiguous topoi, whose names will vary according to the (as yet undetermined) generic context, I think it more prudent to assume that the structure is R: [1, 2(KR), 3(KR), 4(K)].[13] And even the cadential function, though it contains praise of the lady, could be considered as "conflict" in view of the immediately preceding reference to the speaker's exile (III 3-4). Even if he goes off into exile, the speaker will find renunciation painful and indeed impossible. He shall not find that land ("terra" I 3), whose irreality is implicit in the mood of the verb ("u nunca possa seer sabedor / ela de mi nem eu de mha senhor" I 4-5).[14]

# Chapter Two

## i

## Naming Things

In this chapter I shall take up the central thesis of this study: that the first 32 *cantigas d'amigo* in the corpus of Dom Dinis are an organized sequence of poems in whose structure the Renunciation plays a key role. I shall thus be concerned with identifying the genre of each *cantiga*. This will be accomplished in each case by identifying the speaker and addressee (actual, and, if need be, logical), the situation, the topoi, and by analyzing the direction of the sequence of functions. The genres found in this corpus constitute, prior to the reading of them, an unknown set. Each genre must be identified by description and analysis, and then named. The names are arbitrary, and will serve only as convenient indices. In each case, then, genre is an index of the direction of the sequence of functions. My primary concern, however, is to describe and analyze the sequence of genres in the entire set of 32 *cantigas*, and, once the organization of this sequence is demonstrated, to assess its direction.

Throughout this chapter I shall refer to the principal female persona, the "amiga," as "the girl," to her male counterpart, the "amigo," as "the boy". I shall call the female friend of the girl "the girl's female friend," or simply, "the friend." I shall not, then, call either the principal female persona or her male counterpart "friend" although they are referred to in the text in this way ("amiga," "amigo"). A table of speakers and addressees for the entire set of 32 *cantigas* is given in the conclusion.

The words "senhor" ("lady"), "molher" ("woman"), "amado" ("beloved") and "namorado" ("boyfriend") occur in the texts along with "amiga" and "amigo", but although I would retain these distinctions in a translation, I have consistently referred, in the commentaries to the individual *cantigas*, to "boy" and "girl" when speaking of the two principal personae. The age of the personae can be gauged by the nature of the affair. I believe that they should be thought of as young adolescents, in their early teens. Some readers may prefer to think that the young lovers are somewhat older, and of course there is no evidence to contradict such an assumption. The choice is stylistic, and independent of the analysis.

The commentary on each text is limited to an assessment of genre. Where the generic analysis is not problematic, the commentary is correspondingly brief. There are summaries of the sequence of genres after every group of four texts in the first half. In the second half there are occasional references to the developing sequence of genres, but the analysis of the overall sequence is deferred until after the conclusion of the set.

ii

## Criteria

The Portuguese text presented here of the 32 *cantigas* is my own reading of
the text of B (Codex 10991 of the Biblioteca Nacional, Lisboa), one of the two
manuscripts in which these poems are contained. All changes introduced into the
text of B have been noted in the list on pp. 17-18 and are indicated in the Portuguese
text by square brackets. Other than these changes, then, my text is that of B 553-584
(ff. 124r° - 129v°). A table of the corresponding numbers in V (Codex 4803 of the
Biblioteca Vaticana) is given on pp. 18-19. The criteria observed in this modest
"edition" are summarized below.

1. I have not introduced any punctuation or accent marks of any kind.
2. I have removed the capitalization—confined, in general, to the first letter of each
   verse—of B.
3. I have expanded the manuscript abbreviations as follows (in this list the sign $<~>$
   does *not* indicate nasalization, as it does everywhere else in this book—and it
   should be remembered that the symbols used are not accurate representations of
   those found in the manuscripts).

| | | |
|---|---|---|
| p$^r$ | > | por |
| p$^o$ | > | por |
| p' | > | por |
| p̣ | > | per |
| p̣a | > | pera |
| p̣o | > | pero |
| p̣der | > | perder |
| p̣ça | > | perça |
| piurastes | > | periurastes |
| piurado | > | periurado |
| ptirades | > | partirades |
| p$^r$yt | > | preyt |
| p$^r$guntades | > | preguntades |
| porq̣ | > | por que |
| q' | > | que |
| q'r | > | quer |
| q'rer | > | querer |
| q̃ro | > | quero |
| q'redes | > | queredes |
| q'ria | > | queria |
| q'iria | > | queiria |

| | | |
|---|---|---|
| q'ira | > | queira |
| q̃lhi | > | que lhi |
| aq̃l | > | aquel |
| daq̃l | > | daquel |
| busq'y | > | busquey |
| aq̃sto | > | aquesto |
| q̃ | > | quẽ |
| qto | > | quanto |
| q̈to | > | quanto |
| q̃nto | > | quanto |
| Q̈ndo | > | quando |
| q̃ndo | > | quando |
| q̃l | > | qual |
| q'sdes | > | quiserdes |
| q'serdes | > | quiserdes |
| q'sestes | > | quisestes |
| g'sado | > | guisado |
| g'sa | > | guisa |
| g~nd | > | grand |
| at'vera | > | atrevera |
| cat'r | > | catar |
| nenbr~ | > | nenbrar |
| av^r | > | aver |
| av^riam | > | averiam |
| praz^r | > | prazer |
| rog~r | > | rogar |
| viv~ | > | viver |
| avẽt^rar | > | avẽturar |
| o'sara | > | ousara |
| pōco | > | pouco |
| ds~ | > | deus |
| de9 | > | deus |
| se9 | > | seus |
| v9 | > | vos |
| n9 | > | nos |
| d9 | > | dos |
| me9 | > | meus |
| voss9 | > | vossos |
| anb9 | > | anbos |
| p9 | > | pos |
| olh9 | > | olhos |
| falam9 | > | falamos |
| moirem9 | > | moiremus |

| sc̃a | > | sancta |
| nr'o | > | nostro |
| 9 | > | cõ [isolated or at the beginning of a word] |
| ɤ̃ | > | contra |

4. I have not considered the nasal marks in the manuscript as abbreviations, and consequently have not replaced any nasal sign with an "m" or an "n" as the modern editors nearly always do. Instead I have merely indicated the presence of a nasal mark with a til <~> in the appropriate place.

5. I have divided separate words and parts of separate words which are joined together in the manuscript, and joined together parts of the same word which are divided in the manuscript. The matter of word juncture is a difficult one, and although in general I have chosen to regard common combinations such as "por ẽ" and "por que" as individual words, I have decided to treat as one word forms like "daquel," "noutro," "del", etc., as well as some combinations in which the phonetic contour is marked as continuous in the manuscripts, e.g., "nono," "neno," "eno," "guysarlhoey," etc.

6. I have retained the spelling of the manuscript, except in the case of the consonantal "u", which I have given consistently as "v". I have not, however, distinguished between "i" vocalic and "i" consonantal (= "j"), nor have I changed some of the spelling which might be regarded as resulting from errors of the copyists (e.g., "ir" in "poira," "teira," "moiredes").

The only changes which have been made in the text are given in the list below and indicated in the text itself by *square brackets*. Since, of course, the *refram* is normally only copied in full in the manuscript the first time it appears in a *cantiga*, most or all of the *refrans* are frequently printed in square brackets after the first stanza of each poem. Most of the changes made in the text are confined to the change of a single letter, and in most cases this change is based either on an identical line in the text of the same *cantiga* in B, or on the reading of the word in the identical place in V. Occasionally I have chosen to read with B (or both manuscripts) in cases where the modern editors have seen fit to introduce changes. In this sense, and also because of my treatment of capitalization, punctuation, accents, spelling, and nasalization, my text is, I believe, a more conservative text than any heretofore published of these 32 *cantigas* (not counting the diplomatic edition of Monaci, of course). What I have tried to offer is above all a clean text, one which is free of the prejudicial influence of punctuation and accents, and which shows, with a minimum number of necessary alterations (the expansion of the manuscript abbreviations, for instance), what the text of B is. It may be objected that the text is too conservative, since I have not, for instance, regularized the use of the cedilha, nor made certain small changes in spelling (e.g., "pardon" is not given as "perdon" where the manuscript has "pardon"), nor introduced "j" for "i." But my intention is to present a reading of B, and not a critical edition with apparatus. Since several texts are available (Monaci, Braga,

Lang, Nunes, Machado), and since a new critical edition which will supersede them is currently in preparation, I will be forgiven, I hope, for offering so simple an edition of the text of B. Some textual problems are treated in notes to the text, but there is no critical apparatus as such.

## Emendations

| *Cantiga* | *B* | |
|---|---|---|
| 3.8,16 | deyt | d[er]eyt |
| 4.9 | pre | p[o]r |
| 7.10 | por eu | por e[n] |
| 8.4 | vẽ | v[ir] |
| 9.8 | o | o[u] |
| 10.1 | amig9 | amig[o] |
| 10.4 | por eu | por e[n] |
| 10.7 | nos | [v]os |
| 11.3 | sẽ | se[u] |
| 11.10 | pre | p[or] |
| 13.4 | amigo | am[ad]o |
| 13.16-18 | {missing in BV} | |
| 14.11 | pre | p[or] |
| 15.3 | lieto | lie[r]o |
| 15.4 | do | d[e] |
| 16.5 | sabede | sabede[s] |
| 16.13 | amado | am[ig]o |
| 16.17 | vyn | vy[v] |
| 17.10 | vay la | vay la[s] |
| 17.21 | devya | de[s]vya |
| 18.7 | del | d[o] |
| 18.11 | baiorinho | baio[s]inho |
| 18.17 | baiorĩo | baio[s]ĩo |
| 18.21-23 | {missing in BV} | |
| 19.9 | mignado | m[ĩgu]ado |
| 20.1 | cam | c[o]m |
| 20.5 | n9 | n[õ] |
| 20.11,17 | v9 | [nõ] |
| 21.3 | hi fazer | fazer hi |
| 21.5,11,17 | earedes | [f]aredes |
| 21.13 | {missing in BV} | [nõ] |

| 23.9  | ca        | [e] a          |
|-------|-----------|----------------|
| 25.1  | me9       | [d]eus         |
| 25.8  | possededes| po[des]sedes   |
| 27.7  | disseste  | disseste[s]    |
| 27.9  | iuraste   | iuraste[s]     |
| 28.4  | lo        | l[h]o          |
| 28.7  | sofro     | sofr[e]        |
| 29.11 | por amigu | por [vos] amigu|
| 29.15 | amiga     | amig[o]        |
| 29.23 | amig9     | amig[o e]      |
| 30.11 | que veia  | que [o] veia   |
| 30.20 | posse     | p[a]sse        |
| 31.11 | ves       | v[o]s          |
| 32.20 | deyt      | d[er]eyt       |

## iii

## Texts and Analysis

| Cantiga | B      | incipit                               | V      |
|---------|--------|---------------------------------------|--------|
| 1       | B 553  | bẽ entendi meu amigo                  | V 156  |
| 2       | B 554  | amiga muyt a grã sazõ                 | V 157  |
| 3       | B 555  | que trist oi e meu amigo              | V 158  |
| 4       | B 556  | dos que ora son na oste               | V 159  |
| 5       | B 557  | que muyt a ia que nõ veio             | V 160  |
| 6       | B 558  | chegou m or aqui recado               | V 161  |
| 7       | B 559  | o meu amig amiga nõ quer eu           | V 162  |
| 8       | B 560  | amiga bõ grad aia deus                | V 163  |
| 9       | B 561  | vos que vos en vossos cantares meu    | V 164  |
| 10      | B 562  | roga m oie filha o voss amig[o]       | V 165  |
| 11      | B 563  | pesar mi fez meu amigo                | V 166  |
| 12      | B 564  | amiga ssey eu bẽ dunha molher         | V 167  |
| 13      | B 565  | bon dya vi amigo                      | V 168  |
| 14      | B 566  | non chegou madre o meu amigo          | V 169  |

| 15 | B 567       | de que moiredes filha a do corpo velido | V 170 |
| 16 | B 568       | ay flores ay flores do verde pyno       | V 171 |
| 17 | B 569       | levantou ss a velida                    | V 172 |
| 18 | B 570       | amigu e meu amigo                       | V 173 |
| 19 | B 570 (bis) | o voss amigo tã de coraçõ               | V 174 |
| 20 | B 571       | c[o]m ousara parecer ante mi            | V 175 |
| 21 | B 572       | en grave dia senhor que vos oy          | V 176 |
| 22 | B 573       | amiga faço me maravilhada               | V 177 |
| 23 | B 574       | o voss amig amiga vi andar              | V 178 |
| 24 | B 575-6     | amigo queredes vos hir                  | V 179 |
| 25 | B 577       | dizede por [d]eus amigo                 | V 180 |
| 26 | B 578       | non poss eu meu amigo                   | V 181 |
| 27 | B 579       | por deus amigo quẽ cuydaria             | V 182 |
| 28 | B 580       | o meu amigo a de mal assaz              | V 183 |
| 29 | B 581       | meu amigo nõ poss eu guarecer           | V 184 |
| 30 | B 582       | que coyta ouvestes madr e senhor        | V 185 |
| 31 | B 583       | amigu e falss e desleal                 | V 186 |
| 32 | B 584       | meu amigo ven oi aqui                   | V 187 |

# 1

**B 553**

| I.  | 1 | bẽ entendi meu amigo        | 1  |
|-----|---|-----------------------------|----|
|     | 2 | que mui grã pesar ouvestes  | 2  |
|     | 3 | quando falar non podestes   | 3  |
|     | 4 | vos noutro dia comigo       | 4  |
|     | 5 | mays certo seed amigo       | 5  |
|     | 6 | que nõ fuy o vosso pesar    | 6  |
|     | 7 | que s ao meu podess iguar   | 7  |
|     |   |                             |    |
| II. | 1 | muy bẽ soub eu por verdade  | 8  |
|     | 2 | que erades tam coytado      | 9  |
|     | 3 | que non avya recado         | 10 |
|     | 4 | mays amigo aca tornade      | 11 |
|     | 5 | sabede bẽ por verdade       | 12 |
|     | 6 | que nõ fui o vosso [pesar   | 13 |

|      | 7 | que s ao meu podess iguar] | 14 |
|------|---|----------------------------|----|
| III. | 1 | bẽ soub amigo por certo    | 15 |
|      | 2 | que o pesar daquel dia     | 16 |
|      | 3 | vosso que par non avya     | 17 |
|      | 4 | mays pero foy ẽcoberto     | 18 |
|      | 5 | e por ẽ seede certo        | 19 |
|      | 6 | que nõ foy o vosso pesar   | 20 |
|      | 7 | [que s ao meu podess iguar] | 21 |
| IV.  | 1 | ca o meu nõ sse pod osmar  | 22 |
|      | 2 | nẽ eu nono pudi negar      | 23 |

CANTIGA No. 1: bẽ entendi meu amigo

Speaker: Girl

Addressee: Boy

Situation: The girl knows that the boy is very upset because he couldn't speak with her the other day, but he should (she tells him) be certain that his sorrow could not compare with hers. He should return.

Topoi:    1. Boy's suffering (I 2-3; II 2-3; III 2-3; *refram*)
          2. Their misencounter - no message (I 3-4; II 3)
          3. Girl's suffering (*refram, fiinda*)
          4. Girl's invitation (II 4)
          5. Boy's attempt to hide suffering (III 4)
          6. Girl's inability to hide suffering (*fiinda*)

Commentary: The girl refers to an event which took place "the other day" (I 4); the boy could not speak with the girl (I 2-3), and was upset because there was no message (II 2-3). The girl says she knows that the boy suffered greatly (I 1-2, II 1-2, III 1-3), but assures him that her own suffering was greater (*refram, fiinda*), the proof of this being that although he was able to conceal his amorous pains, she was not. In the exact center of the text the girl invites the boy to "return here" ("aca tornade" II 4).

We are not told why the girl was unable to see the boy, nor why there was no message. The text does, however, suggest that a courtship is in progress, and that, despite the unexplained misencounter, the girl is suffering from love-sorrow and is eager for the boy's return. Since there is an explicit invitation ("aca tornade") located in a privileged position at the exact center of the text, I shall assign this poem to a type of discourse which I shall call "Invitation" (capitalized when it refers to the genre and not merely to an act of invitation). The Invitation is the counterpart, within the discourse of the female persona, to the Komos in the discourse of the male persona. The speaker's affirmation of her amorous pains and her invitation to the beloved to come to her are the thematic units which distinguish this genre from such texts as no. 31, which contains neither. The invitation, corresponding to the male speaker's request in the Komos, is not always explicit, just as in the Komos the request may be implied by a sequence of functions; but it is the invitation which is the logical cadential function of the Invitation. Suffering, on the other hand, is a topos which may be found in other genres. It is thus an ambiguous topos, similar to the topos of suffering in male Komoi and Renunciations.

Genre: Invitation

2

B 554

| I. | 1 | amiga muyt a grã sazõ | 1 |
|---|---|---|---|
| | 2 | que se foy daqui cõ el rey | 2 |
| | 3 | meu amigo mays ia cuydei | 3 |
| | 4 | mil vezes no meu coraçõ | 4 |
| | 5 | que algur moireu cõ pesar | 5 |
| | 6 | poys non tornou migo falar | 6 |
| | | | |
| II. | 1 | por que tarda tã muyto la | 7 |
| | 2 | e nunca me tornou veer | 8 |
| | 3 | amiga sy veia praxer | 9 |
| | 4 | mays de mil vezes cuydei ia | 10 |
| | 5 | que algur moireu cõ pesar | 11 |
| | 6 | [poys non tornou migo falar] | 12 |
| | | | |
| III. | 1 | amiga o coraçõ seu | 13 |
| | 2 | era de tornar ced aqui | 14 |
| | 3 | hu visse os meus olhos ẽ mĩ | 15 |
| | 4 | e por en mil vezes cuyd eu | 16 |
| | 5 | que algur moireu cõ pesar | 17 |

6          [poys non tornou migo falar]                    18


CANTIGA No. 2: amiga muyt a grã sazõ[1]

Speaker: Girl

Addressee: Girl's female friend

Situation: The boy, who went off with (in the service of) the king some time ago, has not returned. The girl has thought "a thousand times" that he has died somewhere from sorrow, since he hasn't returned to speak with her, although his intention was to come back soon so that he could see her.

Topoi:      1. Boy's absence (I 1-3; II 1-2)
            2. Girl's fear that the boy has died "elsewhere" with sorrow (I 3-5; II 4-5, III 4-5)
            3. Boy's intention to return (III 1-3)
            4. Boy's delay in returning (I 6; II 1-2, 6)

Commentary: The girl's fear, that the boy may have "died somewhere else with sorrow" since he has not returned to speak with her, will be shown by nos. 5 and 22 to be ironic. She suspects the boy of infidelity. "To die from sorrow" is equivalent to being in love, as is shown by the parallelism in a *cantiga d'amor* (Lang XXVI) of Dom Dinis:

> (I 4)        que andava d'outra namorado
> (II 4)       . . . que eu por outra moiria
> (III 4)      que d'outra eram os desejos meus

The theme of infidelity is mentioned or implied in nos. 5, 12, 14, 16, 22, 27 and 31 in this set of 32 *cantigas d'amigo*, and is also treated explicitly in two other *cantigas d'amigo* by Dom Dinis not in this set (Lang CXVIII, CXIX). In no. 22 of this set similar remarks by the girl are taken as accusations of infidelity (directed against the boy) by her female interlocutor, who responds by defending the boy's loyalty. In no. 5, in a discourse very similar to the present text, the girl emphasizes the boy's tearful promises to return or send a message, and concludes that, since he has neither returned nor sent a message, he must be dead . . . "or he was lying," adding that conclusion in the *fiinda* ("e mort ou mentia").

Though the girl does not, in the present text, explicitly refer to the possibility that the boy was lying, much less to the possibility that he has been unfaithful, the overtones of the *refram* are gradually explained in the *cantigas* mentioned above (nos. 5, 12, 14, 16, 22, 27, 31), so that the irony of her remarks here is retroactively clarified. Since irony is by definition something which is not said textually, it is impossible to document the girl's tone of voice, but the implication is guaranteed by the other *cantigas* in which this theme is treated, especially no. 5 and no. 22 (see the commentary on those texts).

In any event, the girl, though apparently eager for the boy to return, does not express either her amorous suffering or her desire to see him. In this respect, the text can be distinguished from the preceding. And though she does not renounce the boy, her tone is one of anger, which, in future *cantigas* (nos. 5, 20, 27) will lead closer and closer to a renunciation.

Genre: (implied) Renunciation

### 3

**B 555**

| I. | 1 | que trist oi e meu amigo | 1 |
|---|---|---|---|
| | 2 | amiga no seu corazõ | 2 |
| | 3 | ca nõ pode falar migo | 3 |
| | 4 | nen veer me faz grã razõ | 4 |
| | 5 | meu amigo de trist andar | 5 |
| | 6 | poys m el nõ vir e lh eu nenbrar | 6 |
| II. | 1 | trist anda se deus mi valha | 7 |
| | 2 | ca me nõ vyu e d[er]eyt e | 8 |
| | 3 | e por esto faz sen falha | 9 |
| | 4 | muy grã razõ per boa fe | 10 |
| | 5 | meu amigo de trist andar | 11 |
| | 6 | [poys m el nõ vir e lh eu nenbrar] | 12 |
| III. | 1 | d andar triste fax guisado | 13 |
| | 2 | ca o nõ vi nẽ vyo el mi | 14 |
| | 3 | nẽ ar oyo meu mãdado | 15 |
| | 4 | e por en faz grã d[er]eyt i | 16 |
| | 5 | meu amigo de trist andar | 17 |
| | 6 | [poys m el nõ vir e lh eu nenbrar] | 18 |

IV.     1       mays deus come pode durar                            19
        2       que ia nõ moireu con pesar                           20


CANTIGA No. 3: que trist oi e meu amigo[2]

Speaker: Girl

Addressee: Girl's female friend

Situation: The girl tells her girlfriend that her (the girl's) boyfriend is sad because
he can't speak with her or see her, has received no message from her, and is longing
for her. She considers this behavior quite correct. She asks, however, how he can
endure such a plight without dying of love-sorrow.

Topoi:   1.  Boy's suffering (I 1-2, 5; II 1, 5; III 1, 5; implied, *fiinda*)
         2.  Impossibility of boy's seeing or speaking with girl (I 3-4, 6; II 2, 6;
             III 2,6)
         3.  Lack of message from girl (III 3)
         4.  Girl's contentment at boy's suffering (I 4; II 2-4; III 1, 4)
         5.  Girl's suffering (implied, *fiinda*)

Commentary: The interpretation of this *cantiga* can be facilitated by a simple
syntactic analysis.[3]
    There are two main clauses in the first stanza:

                        1) "trist ... e amigo"
                        2) "faz ... razõ"

    There are three main clauses in the second stanza:

                        1) "trist anda"
                        2) "d[er]eyt e"
                        3) "faz ... razõ"

    There are two main clauses in the third stanza:

                        1) "fax guisado"
                        2) "faz ... d[er]eyt"

    There is one main clause in the *fiinda*, which may be considered either
interrogative or exclamatory:

1) "come pode durar"

Of the main clauses contained in the stanzas, five of seven refer to the correctness of the boy's behavior, and this reference occurs with increasing prominence: one of the two main clauses in the first stanza, two of three in the second stanza, and both of the two main clauses in the third stanza make such a reference. This intensification in the expression of the correctness of the boy's suffering directs us to consider her assessment of that correctness the thematic center of the text up until the *fiinda*. In the *fiinda* the rigid pattern of repetition ceases, the lexicon changes, the certainty of the girl's affirmation is displaced by a question, and this question is itself of uncertain import. How do we read this change? Since the *fiinda* often houses the cadential function in a sequence, and since the resolution of the generic direction is frequently incomplete (in terms of an actual and not a theoretical harmony of thematic types), we should not be surprised to find the suggestion of a resolution, and yet not quite the full resolution. The girl's question shows concern, something that she has not shown in the rest of the *cantiga*. Certainly there is no explicit invitation in the text. What we find in the body of the text up until the *fiinda* is syntactically structured on an assertion which seeks to portray itself as unwavering. The tone of the question in the *fiinda* marks the first vacillation within this text in the attitude of the girl, but it is precisely this vacillation which occupies the cadential position in the sequence of functions.

Genre: Vacillation

4

B 556

| | | | |
|---|---|---|---|
| I. | 1 | dos que ora son na oste | 1 |
| | 2 | amiga queiria saber | 2 |
| | 3 | se sse veiran tard ou toste | 3 |
| | 4 | por quanto vos quero dizer | 4 |
| | 5 | por que e la meu amigo | 5 |
| II. | 1 | queiria saber mandado | 6 |

|      |   |                          |    |
|------|---|--------------------------|----|
|      | 2 | dos que ala sõ ca o nõ sey | 7  |
|      | 3 | amiga par deus de grado  | 8  |
|      | 4 | p[or] quanto vos ora direy | 9  |
|      | 5 | por que e ala meu amigo  | 10 |
|      |   |                          |    |
| III. | 1 | e queredes que vos diga  | 11 |
|      | 2 | se deus bõ mandado mi de  | 12 |
|      | 3 | queiria saber amiga      | 13 |
|      | 4 | deles novas vedes por que | 14 |
|      | 5 | por que e ala meu amigo  | 15 |
|      |   |                          |    |
| IV.  | 1 | ca por al nõ volo digo   | 16 |

CANTIGA No. 4: dos que ora son na oste

Speaker: Girl

Addressee: Girl's female friend

Situation: The girl wants to know news of "those who are in the army," namely, whether they will be returning soon or not, the reason being that her boyfriend is among them.

Topoi:     1. Girl's desire for news of boy (I 1-3; II 1-3; III 2-4)
           2. Boy's absence (*refram*)

Commentary: If the girl seemed somewhat harsh towards her absent boyfriend in the preceding text, she has softened her stance here. This *cantiga* consists mainly of a series of emphatic repetitions of her desire to know when he will be coming back. The *refram* ("por que e la meu amigo") states her reason for wanting to know about the return of the army: her boyfriend is really the only one she wants to know about; otherwise she would not be interested (*fiinda*). Her eagerness is shown not only by the repetition of her question, but also by the phrase, "par deus de grado" (II 3): she would like to know news of them "by God, eagerly"; and this phrase occurs in the verse which is exactly at the center of the text. Her eagerness to know when the boy will return is expressed to a female friend, but the logical addressee of the discourse is her boyfriend, and she indirectly declares her desire to see him. It is in this sense that the text can be considered an Invitation. There is no sign of anger, only of a desire to see the boy.[4]

Genre: Invitation

*Summary of Nos. 1-4*

The sequence of genres in the first four *cantigas* is:

> no. 1  Invitation
> no. 2  Renunciation
> no. 3  Vacillation
> no. 4  Invitation

It should be emphasized that the designation "Renunciation" is used to indicate a text in which the movement of the speaker's emotions is towards an anger which could (and later, in similar texts, does) lead to renunciation, whereas "Invitation" is used of those texts in which the girl's attitude towards the boy is affectionate and she declares or implies a desire to see him. It could be argued that in the texts in which she shows anger (nos. 2 and 3) she is angry precisely becauses she is eager to see him, and the angriest of Renunciations can be interpreted as revealing a desire for the renounced beloved. But I am identifying genres based on their thematic logic, not on the psychological motives of the personae.[5]

5

**B 557**

| | | | |
|---|---|---|---|
| I. | 1 | que muyt a ia que nõ veio | 1 |
| | 2 | mandado do meu amigo | 2 |
| | 3 | pero amiga pos migo | 3 |
| | 4 | ben aqui hu m ora seio | 4 |
| | 5 | que logo m envyaria | 5 |
| | 6 | mandad ou s ar tornaria | 6 |
| | | | |
| II. | 1 | muyto mi tarda sẽ falha | 7 |
| | 2 | que nõ veio seu mandado | 8 |
| | 3 | pero ouve m el iurado | 9 |
| | 4 | bẽ aqui se deus mi valha | 10 |
| | 5 | que logo m ẽviaria | 11 |

| 6 | [mandad ou s ar tornaria] | 12 |
|---|---|---|
| III. 1 | e que vos verdade diga | 13 |
| 2 | el seve muyto chorando | 14 |
| 3 | er seve por mi iurando | 15 |
| 4 | hu m agora sei amiga | 16 |
| 5 | que logo m ẽvyaria | 17 |
| 6 | manda[d ou s ar tornaria] | 18 |
| IV. 1 | mays poys nõ vẽ nẽ ẽvya | 19 |
| 2 | mandad e mort ou mentia | 20 |

CANTIGA No. 5: que muyt a ia que nõ veio[6]

Speaker: Girl

Addressee: Girl's female friend

Situation: The girl tells her female friend that it has been a long time that she hasn't received a message from her boyfriend although he swore, crying, when he left, that he would send one at once or return. Since he has done neither, he is either dead or lying.

Topoi:
1. Boy's absence (implied throughout)
2. Boy's failure to send a message or return (I 1-2; II 1-2; fiinda)
3. Boy's promise to send a message or return (I 3-6; II 3-6; III 1-6)
4. Possibility that the boy has died (fiinda 2)
5. Boy's (possible) perjury (fiinda 2)

Commentary: The girl's emphasis on the boy's oaths, delivered amidst tears (III 2), can be seen by the space it occupies in the text—14 of 20 verses. And his tearful insistence on his intention to return or send a message is contrasted with the facts: she has received no word from him whatsoever. The girl's conclusion is that either he must have died—the ironic conclusion reached in no. 2 (refram)—or he was lying. This second possibility, which I have suggested was implicit in no. 2, is reserved until the fiinda, and is the last word in the text. The first overt reference to his perjury thus comes at the end of the first poem of the second group of four in the set of 32. He is openly called a liar in nos. 14, 16, and 27.

Two keynotes in nos. 1-4, "message" (1.10; 3.15; 4.6, 12, 14) and "return" (1.11; 2.6, 8, 12, 14, 18; 4.3) recur here in both the refram and the fiinda.

Although the girl does not renounce the boy in this text, she does not refer to her own (amorous) suffering, invite him to see her, or express any joy with regard to the relationship. The situation contains elements (his broken promises, possible infidelity) which will prompt a renunciation elsewhere in this corpus. A boy's fear of what might happen to him should he return to his girlfriend amidst such circumstances is the subject of one of Dom Dinis's *cantigas d'amor* (Lang XXXIII): he knows that she will "judge him traitor" and reject (renounce) him. We can thus credit the fact that such a set of circumstances could prompt a renunciation on the part of a girl. It is in this sense that the present text can be considered a Renunciation: the sequence of functions implies a renunciatory attitude.

Genre: Renunciation

## 6

**B 558**

| | | | |
|---|---|---|---|
| I. | 1 | chegou m or aqui recado | 1 |
| | 2 | amiga do voss amigo | 2 |
| | 3 | e aquel que falou migo | 3 |
| | 4 | dix mi que e tan coytado | 4 |
| | 5 | que per quanta poss avedes | 5 |
| | 6 | ja o guarir non possedes | 6 |
| II. | 1 | diz que oie tercer dia | 7 |
| | 2 | bẽ lhi partirades morte | 8 |
| | 3 | mays ouv el coyta tã forte | 9 |
| | 4 | e tã coytad er iazia | 10 |
| | 5 | que por quanta poss avedes | 11 |
| | 6 | [ja o guarir non possedes] | 12 |
| III. | 1 | cõ mal que lhi vos fezestes | 13 |
| | 2 | jurou mh amiga fremosa | 14 |
| | 3 | que pero vos poderosa | 15 |
| | 4 | fostes del quanto quisestes | 16 |
| | 5 | que por quanta poss avedes | 17 |
| | 6 | [ja o guarir non possedes] | 18 |

IV.     1      e grã perda perfazedes                        19
        2      hu tal amigo perdedes                         20


CANTIGA No. 6: chegou m or aqui recado[7]

Speaker: Girl's female friend

Addressee: Girl

Situation: A message has come. It is that the boy is dying of love-sorrow and that, no matter what the girl's powers over him, she can no longer heal him. To lose such a boyfriend is a great loss.

Topoi:   1. Boy's message has arrived (I 1-2)
         2. Boy's suffering (I 3-6; II 1-6; III 1-6)
         3. Praise of girl ("amiga fremosa" III 2)
         4. Loss of boyfriend (*fiinda*)

Commentary: This discourse explicitly refers to four distinct personae. "Chegou" ("It has arrived") is the first word of the text. What has arrived is a message from the boy. The message has reached the girl's female friend. In explaining what the message is, this friend says simply "and the one ('aquel' I 3) who spoke with me tells me that he [sc. the boy] is so sad that, no matter how much power you have over him, you can no longer cure him." This message, as we are told, comes from the boy. The message is transmitted first to a male ("aquel"), then to the speaker, who is a friend of the girl (the speaker calls the addressee "amiga" at I 2). We assume she is female because the tradition requires that it be a female voice which speaks first in *cantigas d'amigo*, unless there is a dialog, in which case the female voice should be heard first.

There is one text of Dom Dinis in this set of 32 in which the male speaks first: it is the first text in which his voice is actually heard and is located in the first position in the sixth group of eight. The present text, in which the boy's message first arrives, is the sixth text in the set, and thus the sixth text in the first group of eight. These facts concerning the placement of texts in this set will be adduced later to support my argument that this set is in fact an organized series. The control of the use of the male speaking persona in this set of 32—he speaks only in the sixth and seventh groups of four, in dialogs with the girl—is one of the most salient features of the formal design which I am imputing to the intention of the poet, whether at the time of writing or at any other time during or after the composition of the individual texts.

The girl's female friend, speaking for the first time in the set in this text, is thus the transmitter of a message from the boy to the girl, or rather from a friend of the boy. Whether the description which the girl's friend gives of the boy is to be thought of as her own, that of the boy's friend ("aquel"), or that of the boy himself, makes no difference in the structural analysis of the thematic units in this text. No matter what the girl's (extraordinary) powers (conferred, obviously, by his love of her), she can no longer heal him. The *fiinda*, which has already been seen (nos. 1, 3, 4, 5) to play a key role in generic structure, here marks an important syntactic alteration in the formal presentation of the message. The speaker has heretofore attributed all the information concerning the boy's condition to the intermediary: "aquel que falou migo" (I 3); "dix mi que" (I 4); "diz que" (II 1); "jurou mh" (III 2). In the *fiinda* the speaker breaks this pattern, and says merely, "And you really are losing a lot ('e grã perda perfazedes') when you lose such a friend."

The boy is the logical speaker in this text. In a *cantiga d'amor* of Dom Dinis (Lang I) a boy's voice may be heard uttering such a message as is here transmitted to the girl.

I take pleasure in dying, Lady—
take pleasure because it's bad for you,
for you shall feel what
a lack I shall cause you;
for a lord doesn't lose little
losing the kind of servant
that you lose in losing me.

I take pleasure from my death,
because I know that I shall cause
you the kind of lack a loyal man
(as loyal as can be)
causes the one who loves him (when he's dead);
and you have known perfectly well
that I have been dying like this for you.

And although I must suffer
the most extraordinary death,
my death means nothing to me at all
and I'll tell you why;
because it will be harder for you
to do without my service and my love
than for me to do without life.

And so you may be certain
that though my time shall end
with death (since there's no other way),
I don't intend to suffer for that;
for I shall cause you

> as great a lack as God has ever made
> a vassal cause a lord.

In another *cantiga d'amor* by Dom Dinis (Lang XXVIII) the boy sends off a message with a friend who is going to the land where his lady is. In no. 23 in this set a female friend of the girl tells her that the boy himself has asked her to ask the girl to have mercy on him. In no. 6 then, the logical speaker is the boy, and his discourse, put into the first person, would be this:

1. I am dying of love-sorrow.
2. Not even you can save me now.
3. It will be a shame to lose me.

The lexical interpenetration of the so-called genres of *cantiga d'amigo* and *cantiga d'amor* is sometimes nearly complete.[8] In the present set of texts this occupation of the *cantiga d'amigo* by the male Komos may be held to serve a purpose in the ordering of the texts. The girl was upset in no. 5, and, according to our analysis, on the verge of rejecting the boy. In the present text the girl does seem to have rejected the boy, because he is dying of love and must resort to threats (of his own death) and prophecies ("you'll be sorry if you lose me") in order to try to persuade her to receive him.

Genre: Komos

7

B 559

| | | | |
|---|---|---|---|
| I. | 1 | o meu amig amiga nõ quer eu | 1 |
| | 2 | que aia grã pesar nẽ grã prazer | 2 |
| | 3 | e quer eu este preyt assy trager | 3 |
| | 4 | ca m atrevo tanto no feyto seu | 4 |
| | 5 | nono quero guarir neno matar | 5 |
| | 6 | neno quero de mi desasperar | 6 |

| II. | 1 | ca se lh eu amor mõstrasse bẽ sey | 7 |
| | 2 | que lhi seria end atã grã bẽ | 8 |
| | 3 | que lh averiam d entender por en | 9 |
| | 4 | qual bẽ mi quer e por e[n] esto farey | 10 |
| | 5 | nono quero guarir [neno matar | 11 |
| | 6 | neno quero de mi desasperar] | 12 |
| III. | 1 | e se lhi mostrass algũ desamor | 13 |
| | 2 | non sse podia guardar de morte | 14 |
| | 3 | tant averia en coyta forte | 15 |
| | 4 | mays por eu nõ errar end o melhor | 16 |
| | 5 | nono quero [guarir neno matar | 17 |
| | 6 | neno quero de mi desasperar] | 18 |
| IV. | 1 | e assi sse pode seu tempo passar | 19 |
| | 2 | quando cõ prazer quando cõ pesar | 20 |

CANTIGA No. 7: o meu amig amiga nõ quer eu[9]

Speaker: Girl

Addressee: Girl's female friend

Situation: The girl wants her friend to have neither excessive pain nor excessive pleasure; above all, she doesn't want him to lose hope— the hope that keeps him wooing ("neno quero de mi desasperar"). If she shows him love, he would be so happy that everyone would find out; if she shows him "desamor" ("lack of love"), he'd be so sad he'd die. She wants to do what's best, which, for her, is to have it both ways, that is, keep him in suspense. And so he can pass his time, now "cõ prazer", now "cõ pesar" (alternately with pleasure and pain).

Topoi:    1. Girl's desire to spare boy suffering (I 1-2, 5; II 5; III 5)
2. Girl's refusal to grant boy mercy (I 2, 5; II 5; III 5)
3. Girl's desire to keep boy wooing (I 6; II 6; III 6)
4. Girl's fear of consequences of giving boy her love (II 1-4)
5. Girl's fear of consequences of refusing boy her love (III 1-3)
6. Girl's desire to keep boy in suspense (*passim*; esp. *refram* and *fiinda*)

Commentary: In the last text (no. 6) the girl has been informed that the boy is reportedly on the verge of death, due to his love-sorrow. In this text the girl expresses her wish that he not suffer greatly. At the same time she is wary of showing him favor, for fear that her honor might suffer if the word got out.

The text is explicitly neither a Renunciation nor an Invitation. Inasmuch as she wants to keep him wooing, we can, however, conclude that she is more friendly than hostile to him.

Genre: Vacillation

## 8

**B 560**

| I. | 1 | amiga bõ grad aia deus | 1 |
|----|---|------------------------|---|
|    | 2 | do meu amigo que a mi vẽ | 2 |
|    | 3 | mays podedes creer muy bẽ | 3 |
|    | 4 | quando o v[ir] dos olhos meus | 4 |
|    | 5 | que possa aquel dia veer | 5 |
|    | 6 | que nũca vi mayor prazer | 6 |
| II. | 1 | aia deus ẽde bõ grado | 7 |
|    | 2 | por que o faz vijr aqui | 8 |
|    | 3 | mays podedes creer per mĩ | 9 |
|    | 4 | quand eu vir o namorado | 10 |
|    | 5 | que possa aquel dia veer | 11 |
|    | 6 | [que nũca vi mayor prazer] | 12 |

CANTIGA No. 8: amiga bõ grad aia deus

Speaker: Girl

Addressee: Girl's female friend

Situation: The girl thanks God that her friend is coming. When she sees him it will be the happiest day of her life.

Topoi:     1. Boy's imminent arrival (I 2, 4; II 2, 4)

## 2. Girl's joy (I 1, 3-6; II 1, 2-6)

Commentary: This is the eighth poem in the series, hence marks the quarter point in the set of 32. It is also the shortest text (twelve verses) in the entire set. It is the clearest expression so far of the girl's joy and eagerness to see her boyfriend, who is now called, for the first time, her "namorado" (II 4). The second series of four (nos. 5-8) thus shows a clear sequence: her anger; his komos; her indecision; her joy.

Genre: Invitation

*Summary of Nos. 1-8*

The first eight *cantigas* show the following sequence of genres:

1 Invitation
2 Renunciation
3 Vacillation
4 Invitation
5 Renunciation
6 Komos
7 Vacillation
8 Invitation

Each clear Invitation (nos. 1 and 4, as well as no. 8, whose sequel we will analyze next) is followed by a Renunciation (nos. 2, 5 and 9). After the first Invitation in no. 1 (which has, obviously, no text preceding it), each of the other Invitations is preceded by a Vacillation.

The Invitation in the second group of four *cantigas* is stronger than either of those in the first group, and the Renunciation in the second group is more explicit than that in the first group. Of the four cardinal positions (1, 4, 5, 8) three are occupied by Invitations, one by a Renunciation. The drama represented in these eight *cantigas* can be summarized as follows:

Cantiga no.:
1. She wants him to return.
2. He hasn't come back; she's upset.
3. She's sure he's very sad.
4. She wants news of him.
5. He hasn't come back or sent a message; she's mad.
6. The message has come; he's dying; she'll lose him.
7. She doesn't want to be too kind or too cruel.
8. He's coming; she's overjoyed.

The girl's emotional reaction moves from disappointment (1), to resentment (2), to feigned indifference (3), to eagerness (4), to anger (5), to uncertainty (7), to joy (8). So far the boy has not appeared, and his message arrived for the first time in no. 6. His voice is not heard until no. 21.

9

**B 561**

| I. | 1 | vos que vos en vossos cantares meu | 1 |
|---|---|---|---|
| | 2 | amigo chamades creede bẽ | 2 |
| | 3 | que nõ dou eu por tal enfinta rẽ | 3 |
| | 4 | e por aquesto senhor vos mand eu | 4 |
| | 5 | que bẽ quanto quiserdes des aqui | 5 |
| | 6 | fazer façades enfinta de mi | 6 |
| II. | 1 | ca demo lev essa rẽ que eu der | 7 |
| | 2 | por enfinta fazer o[u] mentir al | 8 |
| | 3 | de mĩ ca me nõ mõta bẽ nẽ mal | 9 |
| | 4 | e por aquesto vos mand eu senhor | 10 |
| | 5 | que bẽ [quanto quiserdes des aqui | 11 |
| | 6 | fazer façades enfinta de mi] | 12 |
| III. | 1 | ca mi nõ tolh a mi rẽ nẽ mi da | 13 |
| | 2 | de ss enfinger de mi mui sẽ razõ | 14 |
| | 3 | ao que eu nũca fiz se mal nõ | 15 |
| | 4 | e por en senhor vos mand ora ia | 16 |
| | 5 | que bẽ quãto quiserdes des aqui | 17 |
| | 6 | [fazer façades enfinta de mi] | 18 |
| IV. | 1 | estade com estades de mĩ | 19 |
| | 2 | e ẽfingede vos bẽ des aqui | 20 |

CANTIGA No. 9: vos que vos en vossos cantares meu

Speaker: Girl

Addressee: Boy

Situation: In his songs the boy has called himself the girl's boyfriend. She claims that this is a boast and a lie, that she doesn't care about him, and is indifferent to his lying. She encourages him to continue to boast and lie as much as he wants to. He will continue to be nothing to her.

Topoi:   1. Boy's claim to be girl's boyfriend (I 1-2)
         2. Girl's assertion that boy's claim is false (I 2-3; II 1-2; III 2)
         3. Girl's claim that she is indifferent (I 3; II 1-3; III 1-2)
         4. Girl's (mocking) suggestion that the boy continue to boast and lie (I 4-6; II 4-6; III 4-6; *fiinda*)
         5. Girl's denial of her love for boy (III 3; *fiinda* 1; implied throughout)

Commentary: The lady doth protest too much. In the previous *cantiga* she was overjoyed at the expectation of his arrival. It would seem that what she said she feared in no. 7 (vv. 7-10) has come about: she has shown him love and he has been unable to contain the secret. She now denounces him as a liar, thereby attempting to clear herself and preserve her honor. The poem shows a negative attitude towards the boy, and is anything but an Invitation.[10] By claiming that his "boast" that he is her boyfriend is a lie she is implicitly renouncing him, whatever her "true" feelings.

Genre: Renunciation

## 10

**B 562**

| I.   | 1 | roga m oie filha o voss amig[o]            | 1  |
|      | 2 | muyt aficado que vos rogasse               | 2  |
|      | 3 | que de vos amar nõ vos pesasse             | 3  |
|      | 4 | e por e[n] vos rogu e vos castigo          | 4  |
|      | 5 | que vos nõ pes de vos el bẽ querer         | 5  |
|      | 6 | mays nõ vos mand i filha mays fazer        | 6  |
|      |   |                                            |    |
| II.  | 1 | e u m estava ẽ [v]os falando               | 7  |
|      | 2 | e m esto que vos digo rogava               | 8  |
|      | 3 | doy me del tam muyto chorava               | 9  |
|      | 4 | e por en filha rogu e mãdo                 | 10 |
|      | 5 | que vos nõ [pes de vos el bẽ querer        | 11 |
|      | 6 | mays nõ vos mand i filha mays fazer]       | 12 |
|      |   |                                            |    |
| III. | 1 | ca de vos el amar de coraçõ                | 13 |
|      | 2 | nõ vei eu rẽ de que vos hi perçades        | 14 |
|      | 3 | sen hi mays aver mays guaahades            | 15 |
|      | 4 | e por esto pola mha beençon                | 16 |
|      | 5 | que vos nõ pes de vos el bẽ querer         | 17 |
|      | 6 | [mays nõ vos mand i filha mays fazer]      | 18 |

CANTIGA No. 10: roga m oie filha o voss amig[o][11]

Speaker: Girl's mother

Addressee: Girl

Situation: The boy has spoken tearfully with the girl's mother, asking that she ask her daughter not to be upset that he loves her. The mother, moved to compassion, does so, adding that she is not asking her daughter to do any more than that. The mother argues that the boy is very sad, and that if he truly loves the girl, she has nothing to lose, in fact, will gain. The mother therefore gives her blessing to the boy's request and advances it.

Topoi:     1.  Boy's suffering ("muyt aficado" I 2; II 3)

2. Boy's (limited) request (I 1-3; II 2)
3. Mother's advice to the girl to cede to the request (I 4-5; II 4-5; III 4-5)
4. Mother's cautionary advice (I 6; II 6; III 6)
5. Mother's compassion for boy's suffering ("doy me del" II 3)

Commentary: After the stern rejection in no. 9, the boy has gone to the girl's mother, asking her to intercede. The situation is similar to that in no. 6, where, confronted with an angry girlfriend, the boy sent a friend of his to speak with a friend of hers, and to deliver his Komos. The mother does as much here, and the topoi represented are typical of a Komos: 1) I'm suffering; 2) I love you truly; 3) You have nothing to lose; 4) At least don't hate me. The difference between a first person Komos containing such elements and the present discourse of the mother is that the mother adds her own warning, which the boy undoubtedly would not have added, that the girl should content herself with accepting the boy's affection—not hate him because he loves her.[12] The tactic works, and in the next poem we find the girl excusing the boy for an unnamed indiscretion.

Genre: Komos

# 11

B 563

| I. | 1 | pesar mi fez meu amigo | 1 |
| | 2 | amiga mays sey eu que nõ | 2 |
| | 3 | cuydou el no se[u] coraçõ | 3 |
| | 4 | de mi pesar ca vos digo | 4 |
| | 5 | que ant el queria moirer | 5 |
| | 6 | ca mi sol hũ pesar fazer | 6 |
| II. | 1 | nõ cuydou que mi pesasse | 7 |
| | 2 | do que fez ca sey eu muy bẽ | 8 |
| | 3 | que do que foy nõ fora rẽ | 9 |
| | 4 | p[or] en sey se eu cuydasse | 10 |

|       |   |                              |    |
|-------|---|------------------------------|----|
|       | 5 | que ant el [queria moirer    | 11 |
|       | 6 | ca mi sol hũ pesar fazer]    | 12 |
|       |   |                              |    |
| III.  | 1 | feze o por encoberta         | 13 |
|       | 2 | ca sey que sse fora matar    | 14 |
|       | 3 | ante que a mĩ fazer pesar    | 15 |
|       | 4 | e por esto soo çerta         | 16 |
|       | 5 | que ant el queria mo[irer    | 17 |
|       | 6 | ca mi sol hũ pesar fazer]    | 18 |
|       |   |                              |    |
| IV.   | 1 | ca de moirer ou de viver     | 19 |
|       | 2 | sab el ca x e no meu poder   | 20 |

CANTIGA No. 11: pesar mi fez meu amigo

Speaker: Girl

Addressee: Girl's female friend

Situation: The boy has upset the girl, but she's certain he didn't mean to, because she knows he'd rather die (kill himself, in fact) than upset her at all. He knows that she holds the power of life and death over him.

Topoi:     1. Boy's indiscretion (I 1-2)
           2. Boy's good intentions (I 2-4; II 1-3; III 1-3)
           3. Boy's service (I 4-6; II 4-6; III 4-6)
           4. Girl's power over boy (*fiinda*)

Commentary: The girl has apparently yielded to her mother's advice (no. 10) and decided to forgive the boy. She defends her decision to her friend by insisting that the boy acted unwittingly. His indiscretion, in our reading, would be to have called himself her boyfriend. The reference would otherwise be vague.[13] The generic sequence **R I V**, seen in nos. 5, 6, 7, repeats itself in nos. 9, 10, 11: Renunciation, followed by a komastic appeal (advanced through a third party), followed by the girl's softening.[14]

Genre: Vacillation

## 12

**B 564**

| | | | |
|---|---|---|---|
| I. | 1 | amiga ssey eu bẽ dunha molher | 1 |
| | 2 | que se trabalha de vosco buscar | 2 |
| | 3 | mal a voss amigo polo matar | 3 |
| | 4 | mays tod aquest amiga ela quer | 4 |
| | 5 | por que nũca cõ el pode poer | 5 |
| | 6 | que o podesse por amig aver | 6 |
| II. | 1 | e busca lhi cõ vosco quanto mal | 7 |
| | 2 | ela mays pode aquesto sei eu | 8 |
| | 3 | e tod aquest ela faz polo seu | 9 |
| | 4 | e por este preyt e non por al | 10 |
| | 5 | por que nũca [cõ el pode poer | 11 |
| | 6 | que o podesse por amig aver] | 12 |
| III. | 1 | ela trabalha sse a grã sazõ | 13 |
| | 2 | de lhi fazer o vosso desamor | 14 |
| | 3 | aver e a ende mui grã sabor | 15 |
| | 4 | e tod est amiga nõ e se nõ | 16 |
| | 5 | por que [nũca cõ el pode poer | 17 |
| | 6 | que o podesse por amig aver] | 18 |
| IV. | 1 | por esto faz ela seu poder | 19 |
| | 2 | pera fazelo cõ vosco perder | 20 |

CANTIGA No. 12: amiga ssey eu bẽ dunha molher

Speaker: Girl's female friend

Addressee: Girl

Situation: Another woman is trying to win the girl's boyfriend and is doing everything she can to get him to stop loving the girl. This, the friend says, is because this other woman has never been able to arrange to have him as her boyfriend.

Topoi: 1. Other woman's attempt to steal boyfriend (implied throughout)

2. Other woman's inability to steal boyfriend (I 4-6; II 3-6; III 4-6)
3. Other woman's attempts to get boy not to love girl (I 1-3; II 1-2; III 1-3; *fiinda*)

Commentary: The boy's campaign against the girl's rejection continues. He lets it be known to her, by an intermediary (the girl's girlfriend), that another woman is pursuing him. By this he hopes to arouse her jealousy and so render her more receptive to his suit. The poem contains a muted threat of renunciation by the boy, but is above all a protest of his fidelity, since the other woman has not been able to win him over. It is thus komastic in intent.

This analysis is confirmed by another text of Dom Dinis, "Nostro senhor, ajades bom grado" (Lang XXVI). In that *cantiga d'amor* the boy thanks God that his girl is now receptive to him, and says that the only reason for this change of heart is that the girl thinks he is in love with someone else. If she knew the truth (how much he loves her) she would never have agreed to receive him.

I shall call this genre "Other Woman" or simply "Other", meaning that it refers to another woman's amorous advances towards the boy.

Genre: Other Woman (Komos)[15]

*Summary of Nos. 1-12*

| (groups of four:) | First | Second | Third |
|---|---|---|---|
| | 1 Invitation | 5 Renunciation | 9 Renunciation |
| | 2 Renunciation | 6 Komos | 10 Komos |
| | 3 Vacillation | 7 Vacillation | 11 Vacillation |
| | 4 Invitation | 8 Invitation | 12 Other |

The sequence **R K V** occupies the first three positions in the second and third groups. In other words, the girl's Renunciation is followed by a Komos (delivered in no. 6 by her friend, in no. 10 by her mother), in response to which her attitude softens and she decides not to renounce the boy. In the second group this sequence is followed by an Invitation. In the third group it is followed by yet another attempt on his part to win her favor, the "Other Woman" poem. Given the sequence in the second group (**R K V I**), we would expect the sequence **R K V OTHER** to be followed (no. 13) by an Invitation. If this were the case, it would also complete the symmetry of genres in the first position in each group, which would thus run (across the top of the chart): **I R R I**. Looking at the poems in second position we could expect, to complete the symmetry, a Renunciation, which would thus form the following pattern in second position across the chart: **R K K R**. That renunciation (in no. 14) is doubly to be expected, since after each Invitation so far has come a

Renunciation. In the third position in the fourth group (no. 15) we would expect yet another a Renunciation, to complete the pattern so far established. Nos. 3, 7, and 11 are all Vacillations, but no. 3 contains a sequence of functions which can be designated as **R > I**, whereas no. 7 is a refusal to renounce or invite, and no. 11 is a refusal to renounce. The pattern is thus V(R > I), V(⌐R, ⌐I), V(⌐R). No. 15, then, should be a text whose sequence of functions corresponds inversely to that of no. 3, and such a sequence would have to be renunciatory with at least a hint of an invitation. Since the fourth position in the fourth group marks the midway point in the set of 32, and so occupies a structurally privileged position, we may expect something unusual and generically complex. All of these expectations, projected solely on the basis of the patterns thus far established, will be fulfilled. Moreover, with the fourth group of four, a new strophic pattern is introduced into the series. The stanzas will be of two lines with a *refram*. And this strophic pattern will, within the group of 32, be found only in the fourth group. This fact helps to confirm the structural importance of the number 4 in the organization of the series (4 groups of 4 in each of the halves of the set).

13

**B 565**

|      |   |                        |    |
|------|---|------------------------|----|
| I.   | 1 | bon dya vi amigo       | 1  |
|      | 2 | poys seu mãdad ey migo | 2  |
|      | 3 | loucana                | 3  |
| II.  | 1 | bõ dia vi am[ad]o      | 4  |
|      | 2 | poys migu ey seu mãdado | 5  |
|      | 3 | louçana                | 6  |
| III. | 1 | poys seu mandad ey migo | 7  |
|      | 2 | rogu eu a deus e digo  | 8  |
|      | 3 | loucana                | 9  |
| IV.  | 1 | poys migo ey seu mandado | 10 |
|      | 2 | rogu eu a deus de grado | 11 |

| 3 | louçana | 12 |
|---|---|---|

| V. | 1 | rogu eu a deus e digo | 13 |
|---|---|---|---|
| | 2 | por aquel meu amigo | 14 |
| | 3 | louçana | 15 |

| VI. | 1 | [rogu eu a deus de grado | 16 |
|---|---|---|---|
| | 2 | por aquel namorado | 17 |
| | 3 | louçana] | 18 |

| VII. | 1 | por aquel meu amigo | 19 |
|---|---|---|---|
| | 2 | que o veia comigo | 20 |
| | 3 | loucana | 21 |

| VIII. | 1 | por aquel namorado | 22 |
|---|---|---|---|
| | 2 | que fosse ia chegado | 23 |
| | 3 | loucana | 24 |

CANTIGA No. 13: bon dya vi amigo[16]

Speaker: Girl

Addressee: Boy

Situation: The girl is happy because she has received a message from the boy. She feels wonderful ("lovely", she says) and prays to God that she can see him. She wishes he were already here.

Topoi:     1. Girl's joy (I 1; II 1; *refram*)
           2. Arrival of boy's message (I 2; II 2; III 1; IV 1)
           3. Girl's invitation (III 2; IV 2; V 1-2; VI 1-2; VII 1-2; VIII 1-2)

Commentary: This is a clear example of the genre of Invitation. It marks the success of the boy's campaign (in nos. 10 and 12), and follows logically on the sequence in the third group of four: **R, K, V, OTHER.** In "Nostro senhor, ajades bom grado" (cited above in the discussion of no. 12) the boy remarks that the girl's change of heart is due solely to her fears that he has another woman. Given the use of this logic in the corpus of Dom Dinis, we may infer that it is at play here. Having feared that she had lost him (the last word of no. 12 is the ominous "perder" 'to lose'), she is more than happy to receive him. We may note that the Invitation, found in the first and fourth positions in the first group, and in the fourth position in the second group, does not occur in the third group, but recurs here in the first position in the fourth group, where, in view of both the linear sequence of genres and the inter-group symmetry, we had expected it.

Genre: Invitation

14

**B 566**

| I. | 1 | non chegou madre o meu amigo | 1 |
| | 2 | e oi est o prazo saydo | 2 |
| | 3 | ay madre moyro d amor | 3 |
| II. | 1 | nõ chegou madr o meu amado | 4 |
| | 2 | e oi est o prazo passado | 5 |
| | 3 | ay madre moiro d amor | 6 |
| III. | 1 | e oi est o prazo saydo | 7 |
| | 2 | por que mẽtio o desmẽtido | 8 |
| | 3 | ay madre [moiro d amor] | 9 |
| IV. | 1 | e oi est o prazo passado | 10 |
| | 2 | p[or] que mentiu o periurado | 11 |
| | 3 | ay madre [moiro d amor] | 12 |
| V. | 1 | e por que mẽtiu o desmẽtido | 13 |
| | 2 | pesa mi poys per si e falido | 14 |
| | 3 | ay madre [moiro d amor] | 15 |
| VI. | 1 | por que mẽtiu o periurado | 16 |
| | 2 | pesa mi poys mẽtiu per seu grado | 17 |
| | 3 | [ay madre moiro d amor] | 18 |

CANTIGA No. 14: non chegou madre o meu amigo[17]

Speaker: Girl

Addressee: Mother

Situation: The boy did not arrive, and the time is up. The girl is dying of love. She asks why he lied. She is in pain.

Topoi:     1. Boy's failure to arrive (I 1; II 1)
           2. The time is up (I 2; II 2; III 1; IV 1)
           3. Girl's sorrow (*refram*; V 2; VI 2)
           4. Boy's perjury (III 2; IV 2; V 1-2; VI 1-2)

Commentary: If we discount the one word *refram* ("louçana" 'lovely'), no. 13 ends "que fosse ia chegado" ("that he had already arrived"), and no. 14 begins "non chegou" ("he hasn't arrived"). The moment of expectation is followed again by a disappointment. This is the fourth occurrence of the sequence **I R**, already seen in nos. 1-2, 4-5, and 8-9. The accusation of perjury, hinted at in no. 2, mentioned once at the end of the no. 5 ("ou mentia") and once in no. 9 ("mentir"), is here found ten times: "mẽtio", "desmẽtido", "mentiu", "periurado", "mẽtiu", "desmẽtido", "e falido," "mẽtiu", "periurado", "mẽtiu." The argument that this is due solely to the use of parallelism is specious: parallelistic repetitions are emphatic.

His perjury and her suffering do not, however, lead to an explicit renunciation.[18] The *refram*, "ay madre moyro d amor," is a declaration of love, or rather love-sorrow, and so implies another topos, that of conflict, seen in the *cantigas d'amor* of Dom Dinis in Chapter One. The poem is nevertheless a Renunciation: the direction of the sequence of functions is signalled by the perjury topos, and there is no actualized modulation to the harmonic sphere of the Invitation.

The use of the Renunciation (in all its gradations) within a series of poems would seem to be governed in part by the principle that the renunciatory elements increase gradually with each use of the genre, and that the explicit renunciations be held in reserve until the end of the series. Although nearly half the poems in this series have renunciatory material, the only explicit renunciations occur in nos. 27, 31, 32.

Genre: Renunciation

15

**B 567**

| I. | 1 | de que moiredes filha a do corpo velido | 1 |
| | 2 | madre moiro d amores que mi deu meu amigo | 2 |
| | 3 | alva e vay lie[r]o | 3 |
| | | | |
| II. | 1 | d[e] que moiredes filha a do corpo louçano | 4 |
| | 2 | madre moiro d amores que mi deu meu amado | 5 |
| | 3 | alva [e vay liero] | 6 |
| | | | |
| III. | 1 | madre moyro d amores que mi deu meu amigo | 7 |
| | 2 | quando vei esta çinta que por seu amor cingo | 8 |
| | 3 | alva [e vay liero] | 9 |
| | | | |
| IV. | 1 | madre moyro d amores que mi deu meu amado | 10 |
| | 2 | quando vei esta çĩta que por seu amor trago | 11 |
| | 3 | alva [e vay liero] | 12 |
| | | | |
| V. | 1 | quando vei esta cĩta que por seu amor çingo | 13 |
| | 2 | e me nẽbra fremosa como falou cõmigo | 14 |
| | 3 | alva [e vay liero] | 15 |
| | | | |
| VI. | 1 | quando vei esta cĩta que por seu amor trago | 16 |
| | 2 | e me nẽbra fremosa como falamos anbos | 17 |
| | 3 | alva [e vay liero] | 18 |

CANTIGA No. 15: de que moiredes filha a do corpo velido[19]

Speakers: Mother, girl

Addressees: Girl, mother

Situation: The mother asks her daughter why she is dying. The daughter answers that she is dying of the love her friend has left her with, especially when she looks at the belt she wears in his honor and remembers the way they used to talk together.

Topoi: Mother's discourse: 1. Girl's suffering (I 1; II 1)

                            2. Girl's beauty (I 1; II 1)
Girl's discourse:     1. Girl's suffering (I 2; II 2; III 1; IV 1)
                            2. Girl's sad memories (III 2; IV 2; V 1-2; VI 1-2)
                            3. Boy's perjury (implied throughout)

Commentary: Once more, the first words of the text pick up the last words of the preceding one: "ay madre moiro d amor"/ "de que moiredes filha..." This observation does not imply that we should imagine the mother as responding directly to the girl's discourse in no. 14. After all, the girl has explained quite clearly in that text why she is dying. The verbal link is structural, not dramatic, and functions in the same way as the link "chegado"/"non chegou" between nos. 13 and 14.

This poem seems less renuciatory than the last. There is no explicit mention of the boy's perjury, and the girl speaks with apparent tenderness of the sash she wears "for his love" and of their conversations together. The topos of "memories" (of the days of love) belongs, however, to the Renunciation.[20] The only other mentions of memories of the past (in the series so far) occur in nos. 2 and 5, and in both of those cases the girl recalls the boy's promises to return. It is precisely these words of love that are evoked in the present text ("como falou cõmigo .... como falamos anbos"), and, given the boy's failure to appear at the appointed time (in no. 14), the girl's recollection of his words of love may be taken as belonging also to the topos of perjury. The girl's discourse, if taken out of the context of the series, would reveal longing and sorrow. Within the context of the sequence it seems to reveal both these *and* a certain bitterness.

I do not believe that the difficulty presented by the *refram* (a double difficulty: of knowing what it says, and of interpreting it within the context of the poem) is accidental. The text, even without the *refram*, is a generic puzzle. It seems to be a principle in riddling texts that the part which should resolve the difficulties created by the rest of the text merely serves to increase the problems of interpretation. "Alva e vay liero" probably means one of two things: 1) it's dawn and (the dawn) goes lightly; 2) it's dawn and he (the boy) goes lightly.[21] The first reading seems unlikely to me because, as far as I can tell, it would be irrelevant. The second reading can be taken as meaning one of two things: 1) it's dawn and my boy is going off light-footed; 2) it's dawn and my boy, who is not here, is going his merry way.

The first of these two possibilities would imply that the lovers have just been together, but that with the dawn the boy has had to leave, and the girl is left lamenting his departure. The first problem in connection with such a reading is what the mother is doing. Are we to imagine her coming to say good morning to her daughter? Does the daughter, then, inform her mother that the boy has just left her? Or are we to imagine (theoretically a sound possibility) that the daughter's response is an aside not addressed to or heard by the mother? All of this is possible, and the poem would thus fit neatly into the genre commonly called *alba*, the lovers' parting at dawn.[22]

Against this interpretation, I would argue: 1) That the daughter is speaking to her mother ("madre moyro. . .") and that it is improbable that she would inform her mother that her boyfriend has just been with her during the night. 2) That the references to the sash worn "for his love," and to their amorous conversations imply the recollection of a time more distant than the immediately preceding moments. While it is perfectly understandable that a lover can feel immediately the absence of a beloved who has just left, and make instant recourse to tokens of affection and recollections of their conversations (and other activities) together, the point of this text seems to be precisely that the boy has not been there, that the girl has only her memories of him, that she has waited the night out thinking of him, alone and dying of love, and that now that it is dawn her sad refrain is: It's dawn (I'm alone), and he is (off somewhere) going (merrily) on his way (forgetful of me).

Until now I have tried, for the most part, to argue from each text towards a unity in the sequence of texts and of genres. I have occasionally used the sequence, as it has been seen to be forming, to interpret difficult passages in individual texts. I shall now resort to such a technique, though merely to reinforce what I have argued above solely on the evidence provided by this text. In no. 13 the girl was waiting joyously for her beloved. In no. 14 he failed to arrive and she was devastated, accusing him of perjury and saying she was dying of love for him. In the present text, no. 15, her anger has been absorbed somewhat by her sorrow, and her accusation of perjury is implicit, not only in her memory of their "words of love" (as in nos. 2 and 5), but also in the ironic refrain, as it has been analyzed above. The logic, then, would be (in the successive stanzas):

| | |
|---|---|
| I and II: | "I'm dying of love for him<br>and he goes his merry way." |
| III and IV: | "I keep looking at this sash I wear for his love<br>and he goes his merry way." |
| V and VI: | "I remember all the words of love he said to me<br>and he goes his merry way." |

Such a reading of the refram is syntactically and semantically certain, and has the added value of making sense both within the text and within the series.

No. 15 thus contains elements of renunciation, but both in its lack of an explicit renunciation and in its emphasis on the girl's fond, if bittersweet, memories it shows a definite conflict on the speaker's part. Of course it may be argued that all Renunciations do, but even within this series we shall encounter several which are much more convincing than this one. Though conflict is common as a topos in Renunciations, it is present here in an elaborate form.

As was seen in Chapter One, in the discussion of two *cantigas d'amor* of Dom Dinis, the generic analysis of Renunciations is most difficult in those cases in which a macrologia of the topos of conflict is expanded to such a point that it seems to represent an included example of the opposite genre (Komos in those cases, Invitation in this), or at least to represent an actualized modulation into the generic structure of the opposing genre. The present text does not seem to me an example of either

of these two types of structure, but rather to contain the topos of conflict in an
elaborate form, which is nonetheless contained within the generic structure of the
Renunciation. If there is bitterness, it is subsumed in suffering; but if there is an
invitation, it is dissolved in irony. Thus neither term would seem to suffice. But,
emphasizing that "Renunciation" and "Invitation" are being used here to denote the
direction of the sequence of functions, I shall designate this text as a Renunciation.

Genre: Renunciation[23]

## 16

### B 568

| I. | 1 | ay flores ay flores do verde pyno | 1 |
| | 2 | se sabedes novas do meu amigo | 2 |
| | 3 | ay deus e hu e | 3 |
| II. | 1 | ay flores ay flores do verde ramo | 4 |
| | 2 | se sabede[s] novas do meu amado | 5 |
| | 3 | ay deus e hu e | 6 |
| III. | 1 | se sabedes novas do meu amigo | 7 |
| | 2 | aquel que mẽtiu do que pos cõmigo | 8 |
| | 3 | ay deus [e hu e] | 9 |
| IV. | 1 | se sabedes novas do meu amado | 10 |
| | 2 | aquel que mẽtiu do que mh a iurado | 11 |
| | 3 | ay deus [e hu e] | 12 |
| V. | 1 | vos me preguntades polo voss am[ig]o | 13 |
| | 2 | e eu bẽ vos digo que e san e vyvo | 14 |
| | 3 | ay deus [e hu e] | 15 |
| VI. | 1 | vos me pregũtades polo voss amado | 16 |
| | 2 | e eu bẽ vos digo que e vy[v] e sano | 17 |

|      | 3 | ay deus [e hu e]                      | 18 |
|------|---|---------------------------------------|----|
| VII. | 1 | e eu bẽ vos digo que e san e vyvo      | 19 |
|      | 2 | e seera vosco ant o prazo saydo       | 20 |
|      | 3 | ay deus [e hu e]                      | 21 |
| VIII.| 1 | e eu bẽ vos digo que e vyv e sano      | 22 |
|      | 2 | e sera vosc ant o prazo passado       | 23 |
|      | 3 | ay deus [e hu e]                      | 24 |

CANTIGA No. 16: ay flores ay flores do verde pyno

Speakers: Girl, unidentified voice

Addressees: Unidentified voice, girl

Situation: The girl asks the flowers of the green pine if they have any news of her boyfriend, about whose whereabouts she is in doubt. She says he has lied to her about what he swore. The unidentified voice responds that he is alive and well and will be with her before the time is up.

Topoi:    Girl's discourse:      1. Boy's absence (implied throughout)
                                 2. Girl's desire for news of boy (I 1-3; II 1-3; III 1,3; IV 1,3; V 3; VI 3; VII 3; VIII 3)
                                 3. Boy's perjury (III 2; IV 2)
          Second discourse:      1. Assurance that boy will return (V 1-2; VI 1-2; VII 1-2; VIII 1-2)

Commentary: This is one of the most famous poems in the entire Galego-Portuguese lyric.[24] Within the set of 32 it occurs in the exact center, at the end of the fourth group of four. The text itself is divided into two halves, each half containing four stanzas of three lines, the third of which is the *refram*, "ay deus e hu e" ("Oh God, where is he?"). It is the only text (in our corpus of 32) in which the addressee is not human (the flowers of the green pine). The second voice cannot be identified with any certainty.[25] It may be that of the flowers themselves, the voice of the speaker's female friend, who is present to her lamentation, or the voice of the boy, conceived of as responding from a distance to the girl's questions. These possibilities (and others) will be discussed below.

   The generic identity of the girl's discourse is not clarified until the second line of the third stanza, with the mention of perjury. In the first stanza it is not clear whether she is uttering a Renunciation or an Invitation. The request for news can (as has been seen) be a topos of both genres. The question "ay deus e hu e" would be ironic in the first case, tender in the second. This polytonality is heightened with the parallelistic variation "amado" II 2 (for "amigo" I 2), but resolved with the mention of perjury at III 2—repeated, with emphasis ("a iurado" for "pos") at IV 2. The genre of the first half of the text is thus Renunciation.

If someone, a female friend of the girl or any other human speaker, is present to the girl's discourse and responds, that person delivers, on behalf of the boy, a discourse which responds to her questions, and constitutes a promise that the boy will return. Such a discourse, containing a promise of fidelity and love-service, would belong to genre Komos. Nor does it matter whether the second discourse (V 1-2, VI 1-2, VII 1-2, VIII 1-2) is conceived of as being uttered mysteriously by the flowers of the pine or by the boy *in absentia*; its generic identity would be the same. The second voice may even be thought of as being the poet's own (not the man, Dom Dinis, but the poet as persona). The *cantiga* which immediately follows the present text, no. 17, is the only poem in the set of 32 in which the sole speaker is not any of the personae of the drama—girl, girl's female friend, mother or boy—but a persona independent of the drama: the persona whom I have above called the poet's voice. It is, to say the least, curious that the present discourse of an unidentified speaker is followed by an entire text whose sole speaker is unidentified, and that these are the only two occurrences of such a phenomenon in the set of 32.

| Genre: | (Girl's discourse) | Renunciation |
|---|---|---|
|        | (Second discourse) | Komos |

## Summary of Nos. 1-16

The sequence of genres moves continually from Invitation to Renunciation and then back toward Invitation. The direction of the sequence of genres is thus cyclical, but its form is triangular: the transition from Invitation to Renunciation is always unmediated (no text intervenes). The transition from Renunciation to Invitation is always effected by means of one or more texts, belonging either to the genre Vacillation, spoken by the girl, or to the genre Komos, spoken on the boy's behalf either by a female friend of the girl or by the girl's mother. The number of texts forming the transition from Renunciation to Invitation increases each time the pattern repeats. One text intervenes the first time, two the second, three the third. The first half of the series ends on the second text of a transition towards Invitation (a text in which the girl is still registering her discourse in renunciatory topoi and the voice which responds to her sings the return of the boy).

The direction of the sequence of affective dispositions shown by the girl in her discourse is from receptivity to rejection, and then, with increasing reluctance, back to receptivity. The cyclic pattern of this movement is constant throughout the first 16 *cantigas* and can be represented by the following diagram:

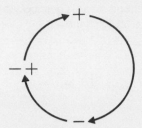

Although the cyclic pattern forbids the designation of an end or a beginning, my analysis suggests that the overall sequence of genres is constituted of overlapping generic microsequences, each of which ends on a renunciation. The first microsequence will, of course, be thought of as beginning with the first text. The other microsequences will be thought of as beginning after each Renunciation.

The first microsequence (*cantigas* nos. 1-2) represents the absolute minimum sequence, and consists of the two genres which are set in binary opposition in the overall discourse of the girl, Invitation and Renunciation. Each microsequence after the first contains at least one other text, found always in the transition towards Invitation. This transition is effected in the second microsequence (*cantigas* nos. 3-5) by one Vacillation (no. 3), the direction of whose sequence of topoi is "renunciation" > "vacillation," reflecting the direction of the sequence of genres in which the text is located. In the third microsequence the transition to Invitation is effected by a Komos (no. 6) and a Vacillation (no. 7); in the fourth sequence it is effected by a Komos (no. 10), a Vacillation (no. 11), and another Komos (no. 12). The fifth microsequence, as yet incomplete when the first half of the series ends, begins with two texts (nos. 15 and 16) which contain vacillating Renunciations (polyvalent sequences, as defined in Chapter One), the second of which is set in a dialog with an unidentified komastic voice.

The basic structure of the microsequences in the first 16 *cantigas* can be represented by the following scheme, which shows in parentheses the positions in which Komoi occur:

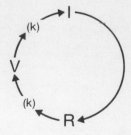

The cyclical, expanding generic microsequences of the first 16 *cantigas* actually form a spiral pattern which can be schematized:

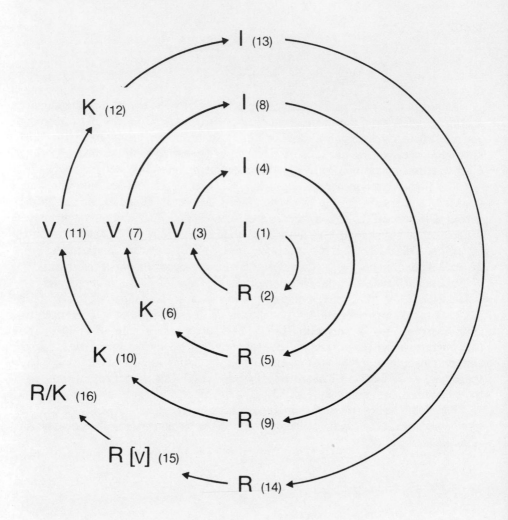

17

**B 569**

| I. | 1 | levantou ss a velida | 1 |
|----|---|----------------------|---|
|    | 2 | levantou ss alva | 2 |
|    | 3 | e vay lavar camisas | 3 |
|    | 4 | eno alto | 4 |
|    | 5 | vay las lavar alva | 5 |

| II. | 1 | levantou ss a louçana | 6 |
|-----|---|------------------------|---|
|     | 2 | levantou ss alva | 7 |
|     | 3 | e vay lavar delgadas | 8 |
|     | 4 | eno alto | 9 |
|     | 5 | vay la[s] lavar [alva] | 10 |

| III. | 1 | vay lavar camisas | 11 |
|------|---|-------------------|----|
|      | 2 | levantou ss alva | 12 |
|      | 3 | o vẽto lhas desvia | 13 |
|      | 4 | eno alto | 14 |
|      | 5 | vay las lavar alva | 15 |

| IV. | 1 | e vay lavar delgadas | 16 |
|-----|---|----------------------|----|
|     | 2 | levantou ss alva | 17 |
|     | 3 | o vẽto lhas levava | 18 |
|     | 4 | eno alto | 19 |
|     | 5 | vay las lavar [alva] | 20 |

| V. | 1 | o vẽto lhas de[s]vya | 21 |
|----|---|----------------------|----|
|    | 2 | levãtou ss alva | 22 |
|    | 3 | meteu ss alva en hira | 23 |
|    | 4 | eno alto | 24 |
|    | 5 | vay las lavar [alva] | 25 |

| VI. | 1 | o vẽto lhas levava | 26 |
|-----|---|---------------------|----|
|     | 2 | levantou ss alva | 27 |
|     | 3 | meteu ss alva en sanha | 28 |
|     | 4 | eno alto | 29 |
|     | 5 | vay las lavar [alva] | 30 |

CANTIGA No. 17: levantou ss a velida[26]

Speaker: Unidentified voice

Addressee: Unidentified

Situation: The girl arose at dawn to wash her clothes in the river. The wind kept carrying them away. The dawn grew angry.

Topoi:    1. The girl awakens at dawn (I 1-2; II 1-2; III 2; IV 2; V 2; VI 2)
          2. The girl washes her clothes at the river in the dawn (I 3-5; II 3-5; III 1,5; IV 1,5; V 5; VI 5)
          3. The wind carries the clothes away (III 3-4; IV 3-4; V 1; VI 1)
          4. The dawn "grows angry" (V 3-4; VI 3-4)

Commentary: This text, which is the first one in the second half of the series of 32 *cantigas*, is distinguished by several features: 1) it is the longest text (30 verses) in the entire set; 2) it is the only text which is spoken in its entirety by an unidentified persona; 3) it is the only text which has a three line *refram* distributed throughout the stanza—in the first, fourth and fifth verses. Moreover, it offers unusual difficulties of interpretation, with regard to both its own meaning and its significance in the series.[27]

It is probable that the girl is either waiting for her boyfriend to arrive and is washing her clothes in preparation for the (sexual) encounter, or that she has just been with the boy and is washing her clothes after having made love with him.[28] The texts immediately preceding and following no. 17 may offer some clue. In no. 16 she was asking where the boy was, and was informed by the unidentified voice that he would soon be with her. In no. 18 she is saying goodbye to the boy. We must conclude that somewhere between no. 16 and no. 18 the boy has appeared, but although this confirms our inference that no. 16 is spoken either before or after their rendezvous, it does not settle the question.

It has been suggested that the fury of the dawn wind is symbolic of sexual arousal.[29] It seems equally possible that it could represent the supposed wrath of the elements at the girl's transgression of the moral code. Such interpretations are at best hazardous. We may try to glean one more clue from the structure of the series. The number of texts required for the transition from Renunciation to Invitation has increased successively in the first half of the series from one to two to three over the course of the first three microsequences. At the end of the first half of the set, the microsequence in progress had occupied two texts and was as yet incomplete. A completion of this cycle before the present text would break the pattern of successive increases in the number of poems required to effect the transition. If, on the other hand, the present text were located before the reunion, it would be the third transitional text. The text would thus serve two purposes relative to the structure of the sequence of genres: 1) it would continue the transitional phase of the microsequence; 2) it would imply the invitation which, though not otherwise explicit at this point in the series, is implicit in the fact that in the next *cantiga* (no. 18) the girl is saying goodbye to the boy in loving tones, bidding him to return. Moreover, an implicitly invitational text of such an intimate character would mark a symmetry between the initial texts in both halves of the set of 32. In *cantiga* no. 1 the girl is waiting for the boy. After four microsequences, replete with misunderstandings, mis- (and missed) encounters, quarrels, temporary reconciliations and renunciations, etc., the girl would thus arrive (in the middle of the fifth microsequence) at the same position, waiting for him to come, but this time in the apparent certainty that she will give herself to him. She would thus begin anew, but at a higher level of intimacy.

All of these considerations lead me to believe that this poem refers to the time immediately preceding the rendezvous. I do not, however, rule out the possibility that it is post-consummation, nor the possibility that, in its polyvalence, it is both pre- and post-consummation.[30]

Genre: Washing

## 18

B 570

| | | | |
|---|---|---|---|
| I. | 1 | amigu e meu amigo | 1 |
| | 2 | valha deus | 2 |
| | 3 | vede la frol do pinho | 3 |
| | 4 | e guysade d andar | 4 |
| II. | 1 | amigu e meu amado | 5 |
| | 2 | valha deus | 6 |
| | 3 | vede la frol d[o] ramo | 7 |
| | 4 | e guysade d andar | 8 |
| III. | 1 | vede la frol do pinho | 9 |
| | 2 | valha deus | 10 |
| | 3 | selad o baio[s]inho | 11 |

|      |   |                      |    |
|------|---|----------------------|----|
|      | 4 | e guysade [d andar]  | 12 |
| IV.  | 1 | vede la frol do ramo | 13 |
|      | 2 | valha deus           | 14 |
|      | 3 | selad o bel cavalo   | 15 |
|      | 4 | e guysade [d andar]  | 16 |
| V.   | 1 | selad o baio[s]ĩo    | 17 |
|      | 2 | valha deus           | 18 |
|      | 3 | treyde vos ay amigo  | 19 |
|      | 4 | e guysade d andar    | 20 |
| VI.  | 1 | [selad o bel cavalo  | 21 |
|      | 2 | valha deus           | 22 |
|      | 3 | treyde vos ay amado  | 23 |
|      | 4 | e guysade d andar]   | 24 |

CANTIGA No. 18: amigu e meu amigo[31]

Speaker: Girl

Addressee: Boy

Situation: The boy is leaving. The girl bids him look at the flower of the pine, saddle his horse, and leave in haste. God be with him.

Topoi:     1. Girl's blessing (I 1-2; II 1-2; III 2; IV 2; V 2; VI 2)
           2. Girl's injunction to look (I 3; II 3; III 1; IV 1)
           3. Girl's injunction to leave (I 4; II 4; III 3-4; IV 3-4; V 3-4; VI 1, 3-4)

Commentary: This text is easily identified as a speech to a departing traveler, and its topoi are among those of the classical Propemptikon: the injunction ("look at the flower of the pine") to "remember our good times together"; the injunction to go; the wish that God speed (favor) the trip.[32] The absence of any schetliasmos ("how can you leave me, o cruel . . .") before the injunction to part suggests that the speaker does not oppose the addressee's intention to leave.[33] It could possibly imply that there is need for haste. If we accept that no. 17 was a description of the girl's preparation for an amorous rendezvous, we would see here her farewell after their encounter. If the encounter took place early in the morning, before, during, or after the washing of the clothes, the farewell could be placed on the same morning, and the need for haste would be explained by the obvious social pressure on the lovers (not to be seen together at such an hour under such circumstances).[34] The Propemptikon is one of the most common and best understood of the classical genres, and there is an example in this series of 32 *cantigas* of another travel genre, the Syntaktikon (which functions in that text as a komastic Renunciation), linked in a dialog with a slim but interesting Propemptikon spoken by the girl, in which the schetliasmos does figure (no. 24).[35]

Genre: Propemptikon

## 19

B 570 (bis)

| | | | |
|---|---|---|---|
| I. | 1 | o voss amigo tã de coraçõ | 1 |
| | 2 | pon ele ẽ vos seus olhos e tã bẽ | 2 |
| | 3 | par deus amiga que nõ sey eu quẽ | 3 |
| | 4 | o vera que nõ entenda que non | 4 |
| | 5 | pod el poder aver d aver prazer | 5 |
| | 6 | de nulha rẽ se nõ de vos veer | 6 |
| II. | 1 | e quẽ bẽ vir com el seus olhos pon | 7 |
| | 2 | en vos amiga quãd ante vos vẽ | 8 |
| | 3 | se xi nõ for mui m[ĩgu]ado de sẽ | 9 |
| | 4 | entender pod ẽ del mui bẽ que nõ | 10 |
| | 5 | pod el poder aver d aver prazer | 11 |
| | 6 | [de nulha rẽ se nõ de vos veer] | 12 |
| III. | 1 | e quãd el vẽ hu vos sodes razõ | 13 |
| | 2 | quer el catar que s encobra e tẽ | 14 |
| | 3 | que s ẽcobre pero nõ lhi val rẽ | 15 |
| | 4 | ca nos seus olhos entẽdẽ que nõ | 16 |
| | 5 | pod el po[der aver d aver prazer | 17 |
| | 6 | de nulha rẽ se nõ de vos veer] | 18 |

CANTIGA No. 19: o voss amigo tã de coraçõ[36]

Speaker: Girl's female friend

Addressee: Girl

Situation: The girl's female friend tells her that when the boy looks at her (the girl), anyone with intelligence could tell that he can only have pleasure in looking at her. She says that when the boy is with the girl he would like to (and should) hide what he feels, but that it's obvious.

Topoi:     1. Boy's love of girl (I 1-6; II 1-6; III 3-6)
           2. Boy's attempt to keep others from discovering his love of girl (III 1-3)

Commentary: The place of this text in the sequence may not at first be obvious. In no. 18 the boy is leaving. In no. 20 the girl will complain that he has not been back for a long time, and come close to renouncing him. In the present text a female friend of the girl pleads the boy's case, just as a female friend has done in no. 6 and (indirectly) in no. 12, and as the mother has done in no. 10, and an unidentified voice in no. 18. A female friend of the girl will do the same in no. 22, after the girl has rejected (or deferred) the boy's own request in no. 21, and a female friend will explicitly deliver the boy's Komos in no. 23, saying that the boy has asked her to ask the girl to have mercy on him, and repeating the boy's words. All of this may help to situate the present text in the story. The boy has gone away. We find out in the next *cantiga* that the girl is angry with him. The present text, in which his case is presented by the female friend of the girl, presupposes the need to convince the girl of the boy's sincerity, that is, presupposes that she is presently angry with him. The sequence of events would thus be: 1) the boy's departure after the rendezvous (no. 18); 2) the boy's failure to return; 3) the girl's declaration of anger and/or renunciation (in some degree).

In my view, it is at this juncture that the girl's female friend delivers the present discourse. It should be noted that in the first half of the series (nos. 1-16) every Invitation was followed immediately by a Renunciation of the boy. In each case the boy did something to offend the girl. Three times he did not appear (the situation in nos. 2, 5, 14), once he divulged the secret of his love (no. 9). In the present situation, after their amorous rendezvous, he has apparently stayed away. And the girl's anger in the next *cantiga* (no. 20) is much more pronounced than in any of the previous poems (nos. 2, 5, 14, 15, 16) in which she complained of his failure to appear. This is understandable on the assumption that, after her apparent surrender to him between nos. 17 and 18, his prolonged absence would be particularly painful to the girl.

Genre: Komos

## 20

**B 571**

| I. | 1 | c[o]m ousara parecer ante mi | 1 |
|----|---|------------------------------|---|
|    | 2 | o meu amig ay amiga por deus | 2 |
|    | 3 | e com ousara catar estes meus | 3 |
|    | 4 | olhos se o deus trouxer per aqui | 4 |
|    | 5 | poys tam muyt a que n[õ] veo veer | 5 |
|    | 6 | my e meus olhos e meu parecer | 6 |

| II. | 1 | amiga ou como ss atrevera | 7 |
|-----|---|---------------------------|---|
|     | 2 | de m ousar sol dos seus olhos catar | 8 |
|     | 3 | se os meus olhos vir hũ pouc alçar | 9 |
|     | 4 | ou no coraçõ como o poira | 10 |
|     | 5 | poys tã muyt a que [nõ] veo veer | 11 |
|     | 6 | [my e meus olhos e meu parecer] | 12 |

| III. | 1 | ca sey que nõ teira el por razõ | 13 |
|------|---|----------------------------------|----|
|      | 2 | como quer que m aia mui grãd amor | 14 |
|      | 3 | de m ousar veer nẽ chamar senhor | 15 |
|      | 4 | nẽ sol nono poira no corazõ | 16 |
|      | 5 | poys tã muyt a que [nõ] vẽo [veer | 17 |
|      | 6 | my e meus olhos e meu parecer] | 18 |

CANTIGA No. 20: c[o]m ousara parecer ante mi[37]

Speaker: Girl

Addressee: Girl's female friend

Situation: The girl asks how the boy will dare to appear before her, or look her in the eyes—if, that is, God ever brings him back—, since he has been away for so long. He will know, she says, that he has no right, no matter how much he loves her, to call her his lady.

Topoi:   1. Boy's absence (*refram*)
         2. Boy's anticipated return and komos (I 1-4; II 1-4; III 1-4)
         3. Girl's anger (implied throughout)

4. Boy's love of girl (III 2)

Commentary: In no. 19 the girl's female friend has said that when the boy is with the girl, his love is obvious. The girl responds here by asking "but how will he dare to look me in the eyes, now that he's been away for so long?" She insists six times (vv. 1 and 4 in each stanza) that the boy would have to be very audacious to dare to return and woo her, adding, in the third stanza, that he himself will know he has no right to call her his lady, no matter how much he loves her ("como quer que m aia mui grãd amor"). She thus responds to the arguments advanced by the female friend in the preceding text. This *cantiga* differs from the other three texts in which she complains of his failure to return (nos. 2, 5, 14, 15, 16) in that she all but says she is unwilling to receive him. But she betrays her willingness in the middle of the second stanza:

> amiga ou como ss atrevera
> de m ousar sol dos seus olhos catar
> se os meus olhos vir hũ pouc alçar

> (Friend, or how will he have the audacity
> to dare even to look at me with his eyes
> if he sees me raise my eyes at all...)

Although she thinks it unseemly that he have the audacity to dare to look at her, she foresees the possibility that she may raise her eyes. Her eyes, presumably, would be looking down out of anger and hurt pride, but possibly also out of a sense of modesty and *pudor*, given the circumstances of their last rendezvous between nos. 17 and 18. In fact, the *amigo* does appear in the next *cantiga*, where he pleads for mercy and the girl answers that she will "do what's best." There follows (no. 21) a dialog between the girl and a female friend which repeats in large part the statement and response of no. 19 and the present text.

One of the *cantigas d'amor* of Dom Dinis has extremely close thematic links with this *cantiga*. In that text (Lang XXXIII) the boy, admitting (in the *refram*) that he has been long absent, wonders how will the girl will treat him, *if God ever brings him back to her eyes*. He fully expects that she will rightfully judge him to be a traitor and says he knows that he has committed a great error. His only hope is that her "mesura" will save him. When the boy appears in no. 21 of this series, declaring his love, and is asked by the girl what she can do, he responds, "[f]aredes mesura contra mi senhor" ("Exercise your *mesura*— sense of compassion—towards me, Lady").

The present text is a Renunciation, the strongest so far delivered by the girl, and expresses an attitude which must logically be anterior to the speech of her female friend in the preceding text. The girl's anger can be evaluated not only by the textual evidence of the *cantiga*, but also by the textual time (five more texts, all of them containing komastic efforts by the boy) required to lead her back to an Invitation (no.26).

Genre: Renunciation

21

**B 572**

| I. | 1 | en grave dla senhor que vos oy | 1 |
|----|---|---------------------------------|---|
|    | 2 | falar e vos virõ estes olhos meus | 2 |
|    | 3 | dized amigo que poss eu fazer hi | 3 |
|    | 4 | en aqueste feyto se vos valha deus | 4 |
|    | 5 | [f]aredes mesura cõtra mi senhor | 5 |
|    | 6 | farey amigo fazẽd eu o melhor | 6 |
| II. | 1 | hu vos en tal ponto eu oy falar | 7 |
|    | 2 | senhor que nõ pudi depoys bẽ aver | 8 |
|    | 3 | amigo quero vos ora preguntar | 9 |
|    | 4 | que mi digades o que posso fazer | 10 |
|    | 5 | [f]aredes mesura contra mi senhor | 11 |
|    | 6 | [farey amigo fazẽd eu o melhor] | 12 |
| III. | 1 | des que vos vi e vos oy falar [nõ] | 13 |
|    | 2 | vi praxer senhor nẽ dormi nẽ folguei | 14 |
|    | 3 | amigo dizede se deus vos pardon | 15 |
|    | 4 | o que eu hi faça ca eu nono sey | 16 |
|    | 5 | [f]aredes mesura contra mi [senhor | 17 |
|    | 6 | farey amigo fazẽd eu o melhor] | 18 |

CANTIGA No. 21: en grave dia senhor que vos oy[39]

Speakers: Boy, girl

Addressees: Girl, boy

Situation: The boy complains that it was a fateful day on which he first saw the girl, that after he heard her speak he could find no pleasure, nor sleep, nor repose. The girl asks what she can do, and the boy responds that she could have mercy on him. She answers that she will, by doing what's best.

Topoi:    Boy's discourse:    1. Boy's love of girl at first sight (I 1-2; II 1; III 1)
                                     2. Boy's suffering (II 2; III 2)
                                     3. Boy's request (I 5; II 5; III 5)
          Girl's discourse:    1. Girl's evasion (I 3-4, 6; II 3-4, 6; III 3-4, 6)

Commentary: It has been noted above (in the discussion of no. 6) that the boy's first textual appearance, in the first poem of the sixth of eight groups of four, corresponds exactly to the first mentioned arrival of his message, in the sixth of the first eight poems.[40] His appearance here has been preceded by two texts in which such an appearance was discussed from the points of view of the girl's female friend, who argued the boy's case, and the girl, who displayed her outrage at his long absence and at the possibility that he might return and dare to court her again. His discourse in the present text is easily identified as a Komos.[41] Her response—she does, apparently, lift up her eyes and respond (cf. no. 20. 9)— is to ask innocently what she can do. When he responds with a request for *mesura* (as the speaker in Lang XXXIII indicates that he intends to do) she answers that she will indeed exercise *mesura*—by "doing what's best." This evasive reply recalls her attitude in no. 7, where to do "o melhor" (what's best) meant neither yielding to his request nor entirely rejecting it.

Genre:          (Boy's discourse)        Komos
                        (Girl's discourse)        Vacillation

22

**B 573**

I.     1     amiga faço me maravilhada     1
       2     como pode meu amigo vyver     2

|     |   |                                  |    |
|-----|---|----------------------------------|----|
|     | 3 | hu os meus olhos nõ podẽ veer    | 3  |
|     | 4 | ou como pod ala fazer tardada    | 4  |
|     | 5 | ca nũca tã grã maravilha vi      | 5  |
|     | 6 | poder meu amigo viver sẽ mi      | 6  |
|     | 7 | e par deus e cousa mui desguisada| 7  |
| II. | 1 | amiga estad ora calada           | 8  |
|     | 2 | hũ pouco e leixad a mĩ dizer     | 9  |
|     | 3 | per quant eu sey cert e poss entẽder | 10 |
|     | 4 | nũca no mũdo foy molher amada    | 11 |
|     | 5 | come vos de voss amigu e assy    | 12 |
|     | 6 | se el tarda sol nõ e culpad i    | 13 |
|     | 7 | se nõ eu quer ẽ ficar por culpada| 14 |
| III.| 1 | ay amiga eu ando tã coytada      | 15 |
|     | 2 | que sol nõ poss ẽ mi tomar prazer| 16 |
|     | 3 | cuydand ẽ como sse pode fazer    | 17 |
|     | 4 | que nõ e ia comigo de tornada    | 18 |
|     | 5 | e par deus por que o nõ vei aqui | 19 |
|     | 6 | que e morto grã sospeyta tom i   | 20 |
|     | 7 | e sse mort e mal dia eu fui nada | 21 |
| IV. | 1 | amiga fremosa e mesurada         | 22 |
|     | 2 | nõ vos digu eu que nõ pode seer  | 23 |
|     | 3 | voss amigo poys hom e de moirer  | 24 |
|     | 4 | mays por deus nõ seyades sospeytada | 25 |
|     | 5 | doutro mal del ca des quand eu nacy | 26 |
|     | 6 | nũca doutr ome tã leal oy        | 27 |
|     | 7 | falar e quẽ end al diz nõ diz nada | 28 |

CANTIGA No. 22: amiga faço me maravilhada

Speakers: Girl, girl's female friend

Addressees: Girl's female friend, girl

Situation: The girl says she is amazed that her boyfriend can survive away from her, that he is so slow in returning. Her friend responds that no woman has ever been loved as much as the girl by her boyfriend, and that he is not to blame for the delay. The girl replies that she is very sad and listless because of the boy's failure to return, and suspects that he may have died. The friend cannot guarantee that this is not the case (since the boy is mortal), but tells the girl not to be suspicious of the boy, because he is the most loyal she has ever heard of.

Topoi:[42]  Girl's discourse:     1. Boy's absence (I 1-3; III 5)
                                  2. Boy's delay in returning (I 4-7; III 4)
                                  3. Girl's suffering (III 1-2)
                                  4. Girl's fear that boy has died (III 5-7)
         Friend's discourse:      1. Boy's love for girl (II 4-5)
                                  2. Boy's innocence (II 6-7)
                                  3. Praise of girl (IV 1)
                                  4. Boy's loyalty (IV 4-7)

Commentary: Rebuffed by the girl in the preceding poem, the boy has apparently
stayed out of sight, further angering the girl. The girl's discourse contains nearly the
same topoi as nos. 2 and 5, has a negative affective direction, and belongs to the
genre Renunciation. Her friend's discourse presents komastic topoi (love, service,
loyalty, praise of the girl) and responds specifically to the veiled accusations of
infidelity. The ironic attack contained in the phrases, "I'm just amazed," "I've never
seen such an amazing thing," "by God, it doesn't make sense," finds a response at II
4-6 in the hyperbolic assertion of the boy's love. The suggestion that the boy may
have died (a suggestion whose irony has already been betrayed by the girl herself at
the end of no. 5) is met first with a countering irony ("I'm not saying he can't have
died, seeing that he is mortal") and then with a response which openly acknowledges
the accusation ("but by God don't suspect him of anything else, because I've never
seen such a faithful man").

   This *cantiga* allows us to confirm inferences about earlier ones. The komastic
discourse of the friend (made on the boy's behalf) shows by its defensive and pleading
posture that the direction of the sequence of topoi in stanzas I and III (the girl's
discourse) is renunciatory.

         Genre:            (Girl's discourse)        Renunciation
                           (Friend's discourse)      Komos

## 23

**B 574**

| I. | 1 | o voss amig amiga vi andar | 1 |
|---|---|---|---|
| | 2 | tam coytado que nũca lhi vi par | 2 |
| | 3 | que adur mi podia ia falar | 3 |
| | 4 | pero quando me vyu disse mh assy | 4 |
| | 5 | ay senhor hyd a mha senhor roguar | 5 |
| | 6 | por deus que aia mercee de mi | 6 |
| II. | 1 | el andava triste muy sẽ sabor | 7 |
| | 2 | come quẽ e tã coytado d amor | 8 |
| | 3 | e perdudo o sen [e] a color | 9 |
| | 4 | pero quando me vyu disse mh assy | 10 |
| | 5 | ay senhor ide rogar mha senhor | 11 |
| | 6 | por deus que aia mercee de mi | 12 |
| III. | 1 | el amiga achei eu andar tal | 13 |
| | 2 | come morto ca e descomunal | 14 |
| | 3 | o mal que sofre a coyta mortal | 15 |
| | 4 | pero quando me vyo disse mh assy | 16 |
| | 5 | senhor rogad a senhor do meu mal | 17 |
| | 6 | por deus que mercee aia de mĩ | 18 |

CANTIGA No. 23: o voss amig amiga vi andar[43]

Speaker: Girl's female friend

Addressee: Girl

Situation: The friend tells the girl that she saw her (the girl's) boyfriend in a peerless sorrow, listless and nearly dead, barely able to speak. But he asked her to go to "his lady" and ask her that in God's name she have mercy on him.

Topoi:[44]  1. Boy's suffering (I 1-2; II 1-2)
2. Boy's inability to speak (I 3)
3. Boy's request to friend (I 4-5; II 4-5; III 4-5)
4. Boy's request to girl (I 6; II 6; III 6)

5. Boy's imminent death (III 1-3)
6. Boy's loss of color, sense (II 3)

Commentary: In no. 9 the girl's mother told the girl that the boy had asked her
to intervene on his behalf and speak with her daughter. Here, finally, the friend
acknowledges that the boy has explicitly asked her to deliver a komastic message
to the girl, and the friend supposedly repeats the message verbatim. By admitting
she has seen the boy, the friend can also give a detailed description of his komastic
suffering: sad, listless, crazed and pale, he seems to be in the throes of death. Yet he
manages to utter his request. The details of male erotic suffering are all found *passim*
in the *cantigas d'amor*. The delegation of these details to the friend's description
frees the boy from having to present them on his own behalf, and his simple Komos
is purified to the limit: "que aia mercee de mi."

This is the fourth Komos delivered by the boy or on his behalf since the
beginning of the current campaign at no. 19. In light of the dramatic development,
we may suppose that the arguments of the friend in no. 22 have not convinced the
girl to accept the boy on his return. He now mopes about town (we are told), wailing
his komoi and sending third parties to soften the ground for the final assault. His
appearance in the next *cantiga* (no. 24), where he declares that he is leaving, must
be seen in this light.

Genre: Komos

## 24

B 575-576

| I. | 1 | amigo queredes vos hir | 1 |
|---|---|---|---|
| | 2 | sy mha senhor ca nõ poss al | 2 |
| | 3 | fazer ca seria meu mal | 3 |
| | 4 | e vosso por end a partir | 4 |
| | 5 | mi cõven daqueste logar | 5 |
| | 6 | mays que grã coyta d endurar | 6 |
| | 7 | mi sera poys me sẽ vos vir | 7 |

| II. | 1 | amigu e de mĩ que sera | 8 |
|---|---|---|---|
| | 2 | ben senhor bõa e de prez | 9 |
| | 3 | e poys m eu for daquesta vez | 10 |
| | 4 | o vosso mui bẽ sse passara | 11 |
| | 5 | mays morte m e de m alõgar | 12 |
| | 6 | de vos e hir m alhur morar | 13 |
| | 7 | mays poys e vos hũa vez ia | 14 |
| III. | 1 | amigu eu sen vos moirerey | 15 |
| | 2 | nono queira deus esso senhor | 16 |
| | 3 | mays poys hu vos fordes nõ for | 17 |
| | 4 | o que moirera eu serey | 18 |
| | 5 | mays quer eu ant o meu passar | 19 |
| | 6 | ca assy do voss avẽturar | 20 |
| | 7 | ca eu sẽ vos de moirer ey | 21 |
| IV. | 1 | queredes mh amigo matar | 22 |
| | 2 | nõ mha senhor: mays por guardar | 23 |
| | 3 | vos mato mi que mho busquey | 24 |

CANTIGA No. 24: amigo queredes vos hir[45]

Speakers: Girl, boy

Addressees: Boy, girl

Situation: The girl asks the boy if he intends to leave. He says he does, in order to spare them both pain, though it will be very painful for him to do so. She asks what will become of her. He assures her she will be fine, though his exile will mean his death, since he can't live without her. She says she will die without him. He says this is not God's wish, and that when he is without her he will be the one to die, but that he prefers his own death to her suffering. She asks if he wants to kill her. He says he does not, but that he is, in effect, going to kill himself by his separation from her.

| Topoi: | Boy's discourse: | 1. Boy's exile (I 2-5; II 3, 5-7; III 3, 7) |
|---|---|---|
| | | 2. Boy's suffering (I 6-7; II 5-6; III 4) |
| | | 3. Boy's inability to renounce (I 6-7; II 5-6; III 3-4) |
| | | 4. Boy's praise of girl (II 2) |
| | | 5. Boy's service (I 2-4; II 7; III 2-7; *fiinda* 2-3) |
| | Girl's discourse: | 1. Girl's suffering (II 1; III 1) |

2. Girl's desire that boy not leave (implied II 1; III 1; *fiinda* 1)

3. Girl's accusation of cruelty (*fiinda* 1)

Commentary: This *cantiga* is quite similar to "Oi mais quer'eu ja leixá-lo trobar", which was analyzed in Chapter One. The text is generically complex. The boy's speech is a Syntaktikon-Renunciation (a speech of a departing traveler which is at the same time a Renunciation) with a komastic motive. The girl's discourse, confined to the first line of each stanza (including the *fiinda*) and thus consisting of a mere four verses, can nonetheless be identified as the schetliasmos of a Propemptikon, that is, the part of a farewell speech (to a departing traveler) which contains an appeal to stay, and an accusation that the traveler's intent to depart is a sign of cruelty towards the speaker.[46] She says: 1) Do you mean to leave? 2) And what will become of me? 3) I will die without you. 4) Do you want to kill me? Significantly, the word "amigo" is present in each of her verses.

In an attempt to arouse pity and provoke an invitation to remain, the boy declares that he intends to leave in order not to incommode the girl with his vexing suit, adding that exile will be death, and working in other komastic topoi—praise of the girl, his devotion (implicit in his desire to leave). The girl softens by degrees: her four verses show a clear logical progression. At the end of the *cantiga* she is protesting that he will kill her if he goes, and he is maintaining resolutely that he is leaving out of devotion to her.

This text marks the 3/4 point in the set of 32 *cantigas*.

| Genre: | (Boy's discourse) | Syntaktikon-Renunciation |
|---|---|---|
| | (Girl's discourse) | Propemptikon |

25

B 577

| I. | 1 | dizede por [d]eus amigo | 1 |
|---|---|---|---|
| | 2 | tamanho bẽ me queredes | 2 |
| | 3 | como vos a mi dizedes | 3 |
| | 4 | sy senhor e mays vos digo | 4 |

|     |   |                              |    |
|-----|---|------------------------------|----|
|     | 5 | nõ cuydo que oi ome quer     | 5  |
|     | 6 | tam grã bẽ no mũd a molher   | 6  |
|     |   |                              |    |
| II. | 1 | non creo que tamanho bẽ      | 7  |
|     | 2 | mi vos po[dess]edes querer   | 8  |
|     | 3 | camanh a mi ides dizer       | 9  |
|     | 4 | sy senhor e mays direy en    | 10 |
|     | 5 | nõ cuydo que oi ome quer     | 11 |
|     | 6 | [tam grã bẽ no mũd a molher] | 12 |
|     |   |                              |    |
| III.| 1 | amigu eu nõ vos creerey      | 13 |
|     | 2 | fe que dev a nostro senhor   | 14 |
|     | 3 | que m avedes tã grand amor   | 15 |
|     | 4 | si senhor e mays vos direy   | 16 |
|     | 5 | nõ cuydo que oi ome quer     | 17 |
|     | 6 | [tam grã bẽ no mũd a molher] | 18 |

CANTIGA No. 25: dizede por [d]eus amigo[47]

Speakers: Girl, boy

Addressees: Boy, girl

Situation: The girl asks the boy, in the name of God, whether he loves her as much as he tells her he does. He says he does, and that he doesn't believe there's a man in the world who loves a woman so much. She says she doesn't believe him, he repeats his assurance.

Topoi:  Girl's discourse:  1. Girl's request for verification of boy's love (I 1-3)
                           2. Girl's reluctance to believe boy loves her so much (II 1-3; III 1-3)
        Boy's discourse:   1. Boy's affirmation of his love of the girl (I 4-6; II 4-6; III 4-6)

Commentary: After the dialog in no. 24, we find the girl questioning the boy, who apparently has not left, as to the veracity of his komastic claims. He responds with a hyperbolic affirmation of his love. She says quite clearly (II 1; III 1) that she doesn't believe he could love her *that* much, swearing, in the third stanza, by the faith she owes to "Our Lord." Unflinching, he repeats his declaration of love.

We see the girl here in a moment of vacillation. Despite her reaction to the boy's supposed intention to leave in no. 24, she is not yet ready to accept him or his claim. In this sense, the affective direction of her discourse here is less positive than in no. 24, but neither is it renunciatory. She seems to be trying to decide what to do. Charting the affective direction of her discourses from no. 20 (Renunciation) to the present text, we see the following pattern:

20.  –
21.  –  +
22.  –
23.
24.  +
25.  –  +

The symmetry of this sequence would be completed by a + in no. 26, and in fact the next text is an Invitation which completes this pattern of affective direction in her discourses (note that the text in which she does not speak—no. 23—comes in the exact center) in the transitional phase of this microsequence.

Genre:          (Girl's discourse)          Vacillation
                (Boy's discourse)          Komos

## 26

**B 578**

| I.  | 1 | non poss eu meu amigo | 1 |
|-----|---|------------------------|----|
|     | 2 | cõ vossa soydade | 2 |
|     | 3 | viver bẽ volo digo | 3 |
|     | 4 | e por esto morade | 4 |
|     | 5 | amigo hu mi possades | 5 |
|     | 6 | falar e me veiades | 6 |
| II. | 1 | nõ poss u vos nõ veio | 7 |
|     | 2 | viver ben o creede | 8 |
|     | 3 | tam muyto vos deseio | 9 |
|     | 4 | e por esto vyvede | 10 |
|     | 5 | ami[go hu mi possades | 11 |

|      | 6  | falar e me veiades]      | 12 |
|------|----|--------------------------|----|
| III. | 1  | naçi ẽ forte ponto       | 13 |
|      | 2  | e amigo partide          | 14 |
|      | 3  | o meu grã mal sẽ cõto     | 15 |
|      | 4  | e por esto guaride       | 16 |
|      | 5  | amigo [hu mi possades    | 17 |
|      | 6  | falar e me veiades]      | 18 |
| IV.  | 1  | guarrey ben o creades    | 19 |
|      | 2  | senhor hu me mãdardes    | 20 |

CANTIGA No. 26: non poss eu meu amigo

Speakers: Girl, boy

Addressees: Boy, girl

Situation: The girl says she cannot live with such yearning ("soydade") and therefore asks the boy to stay where he can speak with her and see her. She desires him so much she can't bear not to see him, and asks him to cure her immense sorrow. In the *fiinda* he assures her that he will live where she tells him to.

Topoi: Girl's discourse: 1. Girl's desire (I 1-3; II 1-3)
2. Girl's plea to boy to live near her (I 4-6; II 4-6; III 4-6)
3. Girl's request that boy cure her sorrow (III 1-3)

Boy's discourse: 1. Boy's service (willingness to live where girl tells him to, *fiinda*)

Commentary: The girl has evidently made up her mind (after her vacillation in the preceding text), declares her love and inability to live in the boy's absence, and requests that he remain where they can be together. The request to "live where you can see me and speak with me" implies that the boy might have left and thus provides a link with no. 24 in which he claimed to be about to depart. She would seem to have yielded to his declarations of love in no. 25, as well as to her own desire ("tam muyto vos deseio" II 3). The boy, as might be expected, is quite willing to remain—according to my analysis of no. 24, he had no intention of leaving and his Syntaktikon-Renunciation was a komastic tactic.

Noting that the girl does not speak in either no. 19 or no. 23 we may now chart the development of her affective disposition from no. 19 to no. 26:

19.
20. –
21. –  +
22. –
23.
24. +
25. –  +
26. +

In these eight *cantigas* all the discourses uttered by someone other than the girl are, in one form or another, komastic. The girl's discourses show the pattern:

20. Renunciation
21. Vacillation
22. Renunciation
24. Propemptikon
25. Vacillation
26. Invitation

Her discourse in no. 24 (four verses), though not an Invitation, shows a positive attitude. The invitation, however, is delayed until no. 26, where she openly asks the boy to stay. The perfect symmetry in the sequence of her affective dispositions is strong evidence that this section has been ordered. The sequence of genres corresponds to an evolving situation in which the girl's strong anger in no. 20 must be slowly mitigated by a complex of wooing strategies on the part of the boy. Just as her Renunciation (no. 20) was the strongest thus far, her Invitation in the present text is the most direct declaration of her love for the boy thus far seen. She has never before told him of her desire (II 3), even if it was implicit in her former Invitations. Neither has she ever before asked him to "cure her measureless sorrow" (III 2-3), an invitation which closely resembles the sort of request found in Komoi by male speakers. Though she has hitherto declared her suffering (no. 1) to him, her clearest revelations of her love-sorrow have always been addressed to her friend or to her mother, and her joy in nos. 8 and 13 was addressed to her friend (no. 8) and to the boy in his absence (no. 13). Here, in a face to face dialog with the boy, she invites him to stay and be her lover.

Genre: Invitation[48]

27

**B 579**

| I. | 1 | por deus amigo quẽ cuydaria | 1 |
|---|---|---|---|
| | 2 | que vos nũca ouvessedes poder | 2 |
| | 3 | de tã longo tenpo sẽ mi viver | 3 |
| | 4 | e des oy mays par sancta maria | 4 |
| | 5 | nũca molher deve bẽ vos digo | 5 |
| | 6 | muyt a creer per iuras d amigo | 6 |
| II. | 1 | disseste[s] mh u vos de mĩ quitastes | 7 |
| | 2 | log aqui serey cõ vosco senhor | 8 |
| | 3 | e iuraste[s] mi polo meu amor | 9 |
| | 4 | e des oy mays poys vos periurastes | 10 |
| | 5 | nũca molher deve bẽ [vos digo | 11 |
| | 6 | muyt a creer per iuras d amigo] | 12 |
| III. | 1 | iurastes m ẽton muyt aficado | 13 |
| | 2 | que logo logo sẽ outro tardar | 14 |
| | 3 | vos queriades pera mi tornar | 15 |
| | 4 | e des oy mays ay meu periurado | 16 |
| | 5 | nunca molher deve bẽ vos digo | 17 |
| | 6 | [muyt a creer per iuras d amigo] | 18 |
| IV. | 1 | e assy farey eu bẽ vos digo | 19 |
| | 2 | por quanto vos passastes comigo | 20 |

CANTIGA No. 27: por deus amigo quẽ cuydaria

Speaker: Girl

Addressee: Boy

Situation: Who would have believed, asks the girl, that the boy could stay away so long? And so, she swears by the Virgin Mary, a woman should never trust the oaths of a boyfriend. She says he told her when he left that he would be right back, swearing by her love, and that he could come back at once since it was his desire to return. Thus, she says, because of what he has done to her, she will never again trust the oaths of a boy.

Topoi:    1. Boy's prolonged absence (I 1-3)
          2. Girl's injunction to all women not to trust boy's oaths[49] (I 4-6; II 5-6;
             III 5-6)
          3. Boy's promise to return (II 1-3; III 1-3)
          4. Boy's perjury (II 4; III 4; implied, *fiinda* 2)
          5. Girl's renunciation of boy (*fiinda* 1)

Commentary: As in every other case so far (nos. 1, 2; nos. 4, 5; nos. 8, 9; nos. 13, 14) the girl's explicit invitation is followed by her renunciation of the boy. And just as her invitation in the preceding text was the warmest so far, her renunciation here is the clearest example thus far of a Renunciation: it is, in fact, the first text which contains the renunciation proper (*fiinda* 1), as well as the first which openly accuses the boy of perjury (*refram*, II 4; III 4). The girl's tone is angry, bitter and sarcastic. She mockingly repeats the boy's own promises to return, enjoins all women never to believe the lies boys tell, and says she will do the same ("assy farey eu bẽ vos digo" *fiinda*).

The violence of this renunciation is proportionate to the warmth of her request in no. 26. We cannot, of course, conclude with any certainty that the boy did not leave immediately, but it would seem highly unlikely, given the duration and intensity of his courtship (six poems between nos. 19 and 25). If her anger after his disappearance following their first rendezvous (cf. no. 17) was such that it took seven texts (nos. 19-25) for her to yield, her response to his prolonged absence after the consummation presumed to have taken place after no. 26 (in which she asks him to "cure" her suffering) is all the more understandable.

Genre: Renunciation

28

B 580

I.    1    o meu amigo a de mal assaz                    1
      2    tant amiga que muyto mal per e               2

|     |   |                                      |     |
|-----|---|--------------------------------------|-----|
|     | 3 | que no mal nõ a mays per boa fe       | 3   |
|     | 4 | e tod aquesto vedes que l[h]o faz     | 4   |
|     | 5 | por que nõ cuyda de mi bẽ aver        | 5   |
|     | 6 | viv en coyta coytado per moirer       | 6   |
|     |   |                                      |     |
| II. | 1 | tanto mal sofr[e] se deus mi pardõ    | 7   |
|     | 2 | que ia eu amiga del doo ey            | 8   |
|     | 3 | e per quanto de ssa fazẽda sey        | 9   |
|     | 4 | tod este mal e por esta razon         | 10  |
|     | 5 | por que non cuyda de mĩ bẽ aver       | 11  |
|     | 6 | [viv en coyta coytado per moirer]     | 12  |
|     |   |                                      |     |
| III.| 1 | moirera desta hu nõ pod aver al       | 13  |
|     | 2 | que toma en ssy tamanho pesar         | 14  |
|     | 3 | que sse nõ pode de morte guardar      | 15  |
|     | 4 | e amiga vẽ lhi tod este mal           | 16  |
|     | 5 | por que nõ cuyda de mĩ [bẽ aver       | 17  |
|     | 6 | viv en coyta coytado per moirer]      | 18  |
|     |   |                                      |     |
| IV. | 1 | ca se cuydasse de mi bẽ aver          | 19  |
|     | 2 | ant el queria vyver ca moirer         | 20  |

CANTIGA No. 28: o meu amigo a de mal assaz

Speaker: Girl

Addressee: Girl's female friend

Situation: The girl tells a female friend that the boy is suffering quite a lot because he will never have her "bẽ" ("good": love). She says he suffers so much that she feels sorry for him, and again ventures the explanation that his sorrow is due to her rejection of him. She says he'll die of the pain, since there is no other possibility. She adds that if he thought he could have her love, he'd rather live than die.

Topoi:    1. Boy's suffering (I 1-3, 6; II 1, 6; III 1-4, 6)
            2. Girl's rejection of boy (I 5; II 5; III 5)
            3. Boy's desire for girl (implied throughout, esp. *fiinda*)
            4. Girl's compassion for boy's suffering ("del doo ey" II 2)

Commentary: Speaking with a friend, the girl seems to revel in the suffering she feels she has inflicted on the boy by rejecting him. Her emphatic description is full of phrases which may well seem ironic: he has "quite a bit" of pain ("a de mal assaz" I 1); "in faith, it couldn't be more" (I 3); "and you see what it is that's doing this to him" (I 4); "as far as I know, there's just one reason for all this pain" (II 3-4); "he'll simply die, since there's no other possibility" (III 1). All of these phrases, as well as the *refram*, seem to show a certain contentment on the girl's part at the the the pain she has imposed on him. She goes so far as to say that she feels sorry for him: "del doo ey." And this is the only suggestion that she is in the least open to the idea of taking pity on him (i.e., receiving him) until the *fiinda*, where she posits the possibility in a conditional manner: if he thought ("cuydasse" is a present contrary to fact condition) he could have her "bẽ," he'd rather live than die.

The boy has been thoroughly rebuffed in the preceding poem. He is pictured in the present text as suffering a mortal pain (III 1-3, *refram*). Since there is no reference to his absence, we may assume that he is again in the vicinity. The girl's description portrays a rejected komast. Her discourse, from her point of view, shows a decidedly negative response to his implied request, though there are two hints (mentioned above) that she is being moved by his agony. In this respect the text is similar to no. 3, where the *amigo*, who had returned after an absence which prompted the moderate renunciation in no. 2, was pictured as wandering around sad, with the girl commenting that his behavior was quite appropriate. In that poem the *fiinda* showed a sudden softening of her smirking anger, and was followed by a *cantiga* (no. 4) in which she revealed her amorous inclinations towards him. The hints of softening in the present text (II 2, *fiinda*) are again preludes to a shift in attitude, seen clearly in the next *cantiga*.

Genre: Vacillation

29

B 581

| | | | |
|---|---|---|---|
| I. | 1 | meu amigo nõ poss eu guarecer | 1 |
| | 2 | sen vos nen vos sẽ mi e que sera | 2 |
| | 3 | de vos mays deus que and o poder a | 3 |
| | 4 | lhi rogu eu que el quera escholher | 4 |
| | 5 | por vos amigo e desy por mi | 5 |
| | 6 | que nõ moirades vos nẽ eu assy | 6 |

| II. | 1 | como moiremus ca nõ a mester | 7 |
| | 2 | de tal vida avermus de passar | 8 |
| | 3 | ca mays vos valiria de vos matar | 9 |
| | 4 | mays deus escolha se a el prouguer | 10 |
| | 5 | por [vos] amigu e desy por mi | 11 |
| | 6 | [que nõ moirades vos nẽ eu assy] | 12 |
| III. | 1 | como moiremus ca ena maior | 13 |
| | 2 | coyta do mũdo nen a mays mortal | 14 |
| | 3 | vivemus amig[o] e no maior mal | 15 |
| | 4 | mays deus escolha come bõ senor | 16 |
| | 5 | por vos amigo e desy [por mi | 17 |
| | 6 | que nõ moirades vos nẽ eu assy] | 18 |
| IV. | 1 | como moiremus ca per bõa fe | 19 |
| | 2 | mui grã tẽp a que este mal passou | 20 |
| | 3 | per nos e passa e muyto durou | 21 |
| | 4 | mays deus escolha come quẽ ele e | 22 |
| | 5 | por vos amig[o e] desy por mi | 23 |
| | 6 | [que nõ moirades vos nẽ eu assy] | 24 |
| V. | 1 | como moiremus e deus ponha hi | 25 |
| | 2 | conselh amigo a vos e a mĩ | 26 |

CANTIGA No. 29: meu amigo nõ poss eu guarecer[50]

Speaker: Girl

Addressee: Boy

Situation: The girl tells the boy she cannot live without him, nor he without her. She asks God to find some way to avoid the death of both lovers. She says they live in the worst mortal pain in the world, adding that it has been going on for some time, repeating her prayer that God decide on some plan for them.

Topoi:
1. Girl's suffering (I 1-2; II 1-3; III 1-3; IV 1-3; *fiinda* 1)
2. Boy's suffering (I 2-3; II 1-3; III 1-3; IV 1-3; *fiinda* 1)
3. Girl's prayer to God for their reconciliation (I 3-6; II 3-6; II I 3-6; IV 3-6; *fiinda*)
4. Duration of their suffering (IV 1-3)

Commentary: The girl admits to her own love-sorrow, presuming upon the boy's, and hopes that God will find a way to ease their suffering. Her mention of the length of time the relationship has been going on is significant: "ca per bõa fe / mui grã tẽp a que este mal passou / per nos e passa e muyto durou" ("For, in good faith, it's a long time that this pain has been going on, and goes on, and it's lasted quite a spell"). This is the first such reference in the entire series and comes in the first poem of the last group of four in the set of 32.

The girl's change in attitude was adumbrated in the preceding text, but though she here implies her own willingness to come to an agreement, she does not openly accede to the boy's implied request. Her repeated prayer to God to find a solution for them is tantamount to a confession that she herself does not know what to do under the circumstances. Still, her confession that she also is dying of sorrow can certainly be read as demonstrating a certain receptivity.

Genre: Invitation

30

**B 582**

| | | | |
|---|---|---|---|
| I. | 1 | que coyta ouvestes madr e senhor | 1 |
| | 2 | de me guardar que nõ possa veer | 2 |
| | 3 | meu amigu e meu bẽ e meu prazer | 3 |
| | 4 | mays se eu posso par nostro senhor | 4 |
| | 5 | que o veia e lhi possa falar | 5 |
| | 6 | guysarlhoey e pes a quẽ pesar | 6 |
| II. | 1 | vos fezestes todo vosso poder | 7 |
| | 2 | madr e senhor de me guardar que nõ | 8 |
| | 3 | visse meu amigu e meu coraçon | 9 |
| | 4 | mays se eu posso a todo meu poder | 10 |
| | 5 | que [o] veia e lhi possa falar | 11 |
| | 6 | [guysarlhoey e pes a quẽ pesar] | 12 |
| III. | 1 | mha morte quisestes madre nõ al | 13 |
| | 2 | quand aguisastes que per nulha rẽ | 14 |

|      |   |                                        |    |
|------|---|----------------------------------------|----|
|      | 3 | eu nõ viss o meu amigu e meu bẽ        | 15 |
|      | 4 | mays se eu posso hu nõ pod aver al     | 16 |
|      | 5 | que o veia e lhi possa falar           | 17 |
|      | 6 | [guysarlhoey e pes a quẽ pesar]        | 18 |
|      |   |                                        |    |
| IV.  | 1 | e sse eu madr esto poss acabar         | 19 |
|      | 2 | o al p[a]sse como poder passar         | 20 |

CANTIGA No. 30: que coyta ouvestes madr e senhor[51]

Speaker: Girl

Addressee: Girl's mother

Situation: The girl accuses her mother of having kept her from seeing the boy, who is her source of pleasure. But if she can, by Our Lord, see him and speak with him, she will, pain whom it may. She says her mother wished her (the girl's) death by trying to prevent her from seeing the boy. If she can arrange to see the boy, she does not care what happens.

Topoi:    1. Mother's prohibition against seeing boy (I 1-3; II 1-3; III 1-3)
          2. Girl's love for boy (I 3; II 3; III 3)
          3. Girl's defiance of mother (I 4-6; II 4-6; III 4-6; *fiinda*)
          4. Girl's suffering (III 1)

Commentary: The mother was the speaker in no. 10, where she advised the girl to be more receptive to the boy (who had come crying to her), was addressed by the girl in no. 14 when the boy had failed to arrive, and spoke two lines in no. 15 (vv. 1, 4), where she asked her daughter why she was dying. Though the mother does not speak in the present text, her attitude towards the boy is (if we can believe the girl) the opposite of what it was in no. 10. She has forbidden the girl to see the boy.

The girl's use of the expressions "meu bẽ e meu prazer" ("my 'good' and my pleasure" I 3), as well as the overall message of the text ("I will see him at any cost"), mark this poem as an Invitation with a substitute addressee (the mother). At the same time, the mother's attitude shows that she, for her part, has already "renounced" the boy, and this implied renunciation (with an implied substitute speaker—the mother) prefigures the girl's own double renunciation in the next two *cantigas*.

Genre: Invitation

31

**B 583**

| I.   | 1 | amigu e falss e desleal          | 1  |
|      | 2 | que prol a de vos trabalhar      | 2  |
|      | 3 | de na mha mercee cobrar          | 3  |
|      | 4 | ca tanto o trouxestes mal        | 4  |
|      | 5 | que nõ ey de vos bẽ fazer        | 5  |
|      | 6 | pero m eu quisesse poder         | 6  |

| II.  | 1 | vos trouxestes o preyt assy      | 7  |
|      | 2 | come quẽ nõ e sabedor            | 8  |
|      | 3 | de bẽ nẽ de prez nẽ d amor       | 9  |
|      | 4 | e por ẽ creede per mĩ            | 10 |
|      | 5 | que nõ ey de v[o]s bẽ fazer      | 11 |
|      | 6 | [pero m eu quisesse poder]       | 12 |

| III. | 1 | caestes ẽ tal caiõ               | 13 |
|      | 2 | que sol cõselho nõ vos sey       | 14 |
|      | 3 | ca ia vos eu desẽparey           | 15 |
|      | 4 | en guisa se deus mi pardõ        | 16 |
|      | 5 | que nõ [ey de vos bẽ fazer       | 17 |
|      | 6 | pero m eu quisesse poder]        | 18 |

CANTIGA No. 31: amigu e falss e desleal

Speaker: Girl

Addressee: Boy

Situation: Accusing the boy of being false and disloyal, the girl informs him that it is no use for him to try to win her mercy: he has acted so badly that she couldn't love him even if she wanted to. He has shown himself ignorant of what constitutes good, worth, and love, has fallen into such a pit that she sees no hope for him, and she will renounce him so thoroughly that, no matter what her feelings, she could never take him back.

Topoi:     1. Boy's perjury (and infidelity) (I 1; implied throughout)

2. Boy's komastic attempts (I 2-3)
3. Boy's unworthiness (I 4; II 1-3; III 1-2)
4. Girl's renunciation of boy (I 5-6; II 5-6; III 3-6)
5. Girl's conflict ("pero m eu quisesse", I 6; II 6; III 6)

Commentary: The boy has been called a liar by implication (no. 2) and openly (nos. 5, 9, 14, 16, 27). He has been called "desmêtido" (no. 14), "periurado" (nos. 14, 27), and has been rebuked in all of the Renunciations thus far in the series. But none of them has opened so strongly as this one, nor has he ever been called "falss[o]" or "desleal," adjectives with which he is reviled in the first verse of the present text.[52] If the renunciation proper was implicit in no. 27 ("assy farey eu," *fiinda*), it is explicit in this text in the *refram* and in the simple phrase "ca ia vos eu desêparey" ("for I shall from this moment renounce you"). It is implied that the boy has come a-wooing (I 2-3, "que prol a de vos trabalhar / de na mha mercee cobrar" 'What good does it do you to trouble yourself to try to win my mercy'), but it is no use: he has shown by his actions that he knows nothing of love (II 1-3). The emphasis on his bad behavior (I 1, 4; II 1-3; III 1-2), the suddenness of the opening rebuke, the reiteration of the renunciation (four times), and the added warning that nothing, not even the girl's own love — should she henceforth feel any for him—could make her change her mind, all mark this as the strongest Renunciation so far in this series.

What, we may ask, has he done? In no. 30 the girl, speaking with her mother, was prepared to see the boy at any cost, although the mother had prohibited her from doing so. What has made her change her mind?[53] We could try to supply a dramatic development understood to have taken place between the preceding text and the present one, for instance, that the boy has again reaped the fruits of love and then abandoned the girl, so that her present fury would be the greeting he would receive on his return. Such an inference (or any similar one which would account for the transition) would be a matter of imagination, and would not admit of any proof. Since this sequence of events seems to have taken place before (between nos. 18 and 19, and again between nos. 26 and 27), there is reason to suspect that is has occurred again here. But there are two other possibilities: 1) that the mother knew something which the daughter did not, and in response to the daughter's discourse in no. 30 informed her; 2) that the girl has discovered that the boy has another girlfriend. These two possibilities are not mutually exclusive, since the information which the mother might have shared with the daughter in order to prevent her from seeing the boy could have been the fact that the boy was involved with someone else. If the daughter discovered this for herself or was told by the mother, she does not explicitly mention it in the present text. But the repeated, emphatic references to something the boy has done, starting with the adjectives "false" and "disloyal," could well refer to infidelity, and the girl's failure to specify the crime may be attributed to delicacy or to pride. Infidelity is not explicitly mentioned anywhere in this series, though in no. 12 a friend of the girl tells her that another woman is after the boy. I have analyzed that text as being komastic in nature, and Lang XXVI supports this view. Infidelity *is* specifically mentioned in *cantigas d'amigo* of Dom Dinis, however. In Lang CXVIII a female friend of the girl informs her that her boyfriend is in the clutches of another girl.

> Your friend, o friend,
> whom you trust so much,
> I'd like you to know
> that a woman whom God should curse
>     has got him crazy and bewitched
>     and I'm dying of hatred.
>
> I'm not going to hide anything from you
> or keep anything secret;
> but you should know for certain
> that a woman whom God should confound
>     has got him crazy and bewitched
>     and I'm dying of hatred.
>
> I don't know any woman who takes joy
> in stealing their boyfriends
> from other girls, and so I'm telling you
> that a woman whom God should destroy
>     has got him crazy and bewitched
>     and I'm dying of hatred.

And in the *cantiga* which follows (Lang CXIX) the girl begins:

> False friend, lacking loyalty,
> Now I see the great falsity
> with which you've treated me for a long time;
> for I know, in truth, of another
> to whom you've tossed that rock.

In these two texts the mention of another woman is explicit and emphatic. The second text (CXIX) begins almost exactly like no. 31: "Ai fals' amigu' e sem lealdade!" The word "falso" occurs in the corpus of Dom Dinis only in these two poems (no. 31 and CXIX) and the word "falsidade" occurs only in CXIX (vv. 2, 17). Thus, of the four occurrences of "falso," three are explicit references to infidelity, occurring in the first verse of each of the stanzas of CXIX; and both of the occurrences of "falsidade" are explicit references to infidelity. That leaves only the occurrence in no. 31. In view of the above parallels, and given the gravity of the boy's offense ("You have fallen in such a fall")[54] and the girl's obvious revulsion, it is not unlikely that she has discovered that her boyfriend has been with another girl.

Genre: Renunciation

32

**B 584**

| I. | 1 | meu amigo ven oi aqui | 1 |
|----|---|-----------------------|---|
|    | 2 | e diz que quer migo falar | 2 |
|    | 3 | e sab el que mi faz pesar | 3 |
|    | 4 | madre poys que lhi eu defendi | 4 |
|    | 5 | que nõ fosse per nulha rẽ | 5 |
|    | 6 | per hu eu foss e ora vẽ | 6 |

| II. | 1 | aqui e foy pecado seu | 7 |
|-----|---|-----------------------|---|
|     | 2 | de sol poner no coraçõ | 8 |
|     | 3 | madre passar mha defenssõ | 9 |
|     | 4 | ca sab el que lhi mandey eu | 10 |
|     | 5 | que nõ fosse per nulha rẽ | 11 |
|     | 6 | [per hu eu foss e ora vẽ] | 12 |

| III. | 1 | aqui hu eu cõ el faley | 13 |
|------|---|-----------------------|----|
|      | 2 | per ante vos madr e senhor | 14 |
|      | 3 | e oy mays perde meu amor | 15 |
|      | 4 | pois lh eu defendi e mandey | 16 |
|      | 5 | que nõ fosse per nulha ren | 17 |
|      | 6 | [per hu eu foss e ora vẽ] | 18 |

| IV. | 1 | aqui madr e poys fez mal sen | 19 |
|-----|---|------------------------------|----|
|     | 2 | d[er]eyt e que perça meu bẽ | 20 |

CANTIGA No. 32: meu amigo ven oi aqui[55]

Speaker: Girl

Addressee: Mother

Situation: The girl tells her mother that the boy has come to speak with her, though he knows it bothers her and he has been forbidden to appear under any circumstances. Since he has come back despite her warning, he has utterly lost her, as is only right.

Topoi:      1. Boy's komastic attempts (I 1-2)
            2. Girl's distress (I 3)
            3. Girl's prohibition (that boy not come) (I 4-6; II 3-6; III 4-6)
            4. Boy's violation of girl's prohibition (I 6-II 3; II 6-III 1; III 6-*fiinda* 1)
            5. Girl's renunciation of boy (III 3; *fiinda* 2)

Commentary: Despite her renunciation in no. 31, the boy (perhaps seeing room for hope in her words, "I couldn't love you, *even if I wanted to*," no. 31 *refram*) has returned. The girl, who had apparently instructed him not to appear ("per nulha rẽ" 'no matter what' 'for any reason'), is firm in her resolve and tells her mother that he has "lost her love." The mother, who had already forbidden the girl to see the boy in no. 30, is presumably content with her daughter's decision, and the daughter seems pleased to inform the mother of it, secure in the knowledge that her mother will approve. The boy has thus been twice rebuffed in his attempt to continue the courtship (cf. no. 31.2-3).

The girl refers in this text to a previous renunciation—her orders that the boy not come to see her—and proceeds to utter another one. The renunciation proper appears twice, at III 3 and in the last verse of the poem. The first of these, at III 3, occurs in precisely the same position (the third verse of the third of three stanzas of six verses) as her renunciation in no. 31 ("ca ia vos eu desẽparey"). But the renunciation in the present text is even more explicit:

> (III 3) e oy mais perde meu amor
> (from now on he's lost my love)

The renunciation is repeated, in a slightly altered form, in the last verse of the *fiinda*:

> d[er]eyt e que perça meu bẽ
> (it's right that he lose my love)

Thus the series ends with what is perhaps the clearest example of a Renunciation in the entire set of 32 *cantigas*.

Genre: Renunciation

# Chapter Three

In demonstrating the structural integrity of this set of 32 *cantigas d'amigo*, I shall base my arguments on four criteria:

1. the distribution of personae as speaker and addressee;
2. the sequence of genres;
3. the sequence of affective dispositions in the attitudes of the girl;
4. the symmetries of generic forms and affective dispositions (on the girl's part) seen in the division of texts into groups of four, eight and sixteen, that is, into eighths, quarters, and halves.

I shall now consider these criteria one by one in relation to the entire series.

## 1. Distribution of the Personae as Speaker and Addressee:

The personae in the drama are:

1) the girl
2) the boy
3) the girl's female friend (considered here, for convenience, as a single persona)
4) the mother
5) an unidentified voice (in no. 16 V-VIII, and no. 17).

The distribution of these personae as speaker and/or addressee in the 32 texts is shown in the following table:

| Text # | Speaker | Addressee |
|--------|---------|-----------|
| 1 | girl | boy |
| 2 | girl | friend |
| 3 | girl | friend |
| 4 | girl | friend |
| 5 | girl | friend |
| 6 | friend | girl |
| 7 | girl | friend |
| 8 | girl | friend |
| 9 | girl | boy |
| 10 | mother | girl |
| 11 | girl | friend |
| 12 | friend | girl |
| 13 | girl | boy |
| 14 | girl | mother |
| 15 | mother / girl | |

| 16 | girl / ? | |
| 17 | ? | - |
| 18 | girl | boy |
| 19 | friend | girl |
| 20 | girl | friend |
| 21 | boy / girl | |
| 22 | girl / friend | |
| 23 | friend | girl |
| 24 | girl / boy | |
| 25 | girl / boy | |
| 26 | girl / boy | |
| 27 | girl | boy |
| 28 | girl | friend |
| 29 | girl | boy |
| 30 | girl | mother |
| 31 | girl | boy |
| 32 | girl | mother |

* dialogs are marked with a / between the two participants, who serve as both speaker and addressee.

? indicates an unidentified speaker

In nos. 23 and 27, the boy's words are quoted by the speaker.

---

The variations, with the number of occurrences, are given below. The totals are followed in parentheses by the numbers of the texts in which the configuration occurs:

| MONOLOGS: | Girl [to friend] | 9 (2,3,4,5,7,8,11,20,28) |
| | Girl [to boy] | 7 (1,9,13,18,27,29,31) |
| | Friend [to girl] | 4 (5,12,19,23) |
| | Girl [to mother] | 3 (14,30,32) |
| | Mother [to girl] | 1 (10) |
| | | |
| DIALOGS | Girl / Boy | 4 (21,24,25,26) |
| | Girl / Mother | 1 (15) |
| | Girl / Friend | 1 (22) |
| | Girl / ? | 1 (16) |
| | | |
| ANOMALOUS | ? | 1 (17) |
| | | |
| | TOTAL | 32 |

Several observations can be made about the distribution of each of the personae

as speaker and addressee. In the tables given below each number indicates the number of times *per group of four texts* that the persona is used in the indicated role.
1) The texts in which the girl figures as speaker are distributed by groups of four as follows:

| | | | | | | | | |
|---|---|---|---|---|---|---|---|---|
| Speaker | 4 | 3 | 2 | 4 | 2 | 3 | 4 | 4 |
| Sole Speaker | 4 | 3 | 2 | 2 | 2 | 0 | 2 | 4 |
| Addressee | 0 | 1 | 2 | 2 | 1 | 3 | 2 | 0 |

The girl is a speaker in thirteen of sixteen texts in each half. In the last two groups of the second half she speaks in every text. She is sole speaker in all four texts in the first and last groups of the series.
2) The friend figures as sole speaker in four texts, distributed as follows:

$$0 \quad 1 \quad 1 \quad 0 \qquad\qquad 1 \quad 1 \quad 0 \quad 0$$

The friend figures as addressee in ten texts (one of which is a dialog in which she also speaks):

$$3 \quad 3 \quad 1 \quad 0 \qquad\qquad 1 \quad 1 \quad 1 \quad 0$$

The friend does not figure as speaker or addressee in any text in the last group in either half, although she figures in all of the other groups as speaker or addressee. Her total participation (as speaker and/or addressee) is distributed:

$$3 \quad 4 \quad 2 \quad 0 \qquad\qquad 2 \quad 2 \quad 1 \quad 0$$

3) The mother is sole speaker in one text (no. 10), speaks two verses in a partial dialog with the girl in one text (no. 15), and is addressee in that text, as well as in three others (nos. 14,30,32). The distribution of these texts in which she figures is as follows:

$$0 \quad 0 \quad 1 \quad 2 \qquad\qquad 0 \quad 0 \quad 0 \quad 2$$

She figures twice in the last group of each half. Her other appearance is as sole speaker in the third group, position 2. She is the addressee of the last poem.
4) The boy does not speak in the first half. He is, however, addressed by the girl three times; each of these texts occupies the first position in its respective group, as follows:

$$1 \quad 0 \quad 1 \quad 1$$

In four texts in the second half he is addressed but does not speak:

$$1 \quad 0 \quad 1 \quad 2$$

He thus figures as addressee (discounting the dialogs in which he takes part) in a total of seven texts, distributed as follows:

$$1 \quad 0 \quad 1 \quad 1 \qquad\qquad 1 \quad 0 \quad 1 \quad 2$$

The boy takes part in four dialogs, all of them in the sixth and seventh groups. In the first and third of these dialogs (nos. 21 and 25) the division of lines between boy and girl is equal (three vv. for each in each stanza). In the second of the four dialogs (no. 24), he speaks six of seven lines in each stanza and two of three in the *fiinda*. In the fourth of these four dialogs (no. 26), he speaks only the two line *fiinda*: the rest of the text is spoken by the girl. His participation as speaker is distributed as follows:

$$0 \quad 0 \quad 0 \quad 0 \qquad\qquad 0 \quad 2 \quad 2 \quad 0$$

The first and third of these dialogs occupy the first position in the sixth and seventh groups, respectively. The fourth of these dialogs (no. 26, in which the boy utters only two verses) occupies the second position in the seventh group. The third dialog, the one in which the boy figures most prominently, occupies the last position in the sixth group, and thus comes at the end of the third quarter of the entire series.

5) The texts in which an unidentified voice figures (nos. 16 and 17) are located in the last position in the last group in the first half, and in the first position in the first group in the second half, that is, on either side of the juncture of the two halves of the series.

From the foregoing we may note the following salient features in the distribution of personae:[1]

1) The girl figures as speaker in 13 texts in each half.
2) The girl is the sole speaker in all four texts in the first and last groups of the series.
3) The friend is the sole speaker in two texts in each half, once in each of two groups.
4) The friend does not figure as speaker or addressee in the last group of either half.
5) The boy figures as addressee, but not speaker, once in each but the second group in each half, twice in the last group of the second half. In the first half he is addressed only in the first position.
6) The boy does not speak in the first half.
7) The boy speaks in four dialogs in the second half: two in each of groups six and seven. The two dialogs in which he participates equally are located in the first position. The dialog in which he speaks only two verses is located in the second

position in the seventh group (and is the last time he speaks). The dialog in which he dominates is in the last position in group six, at the end of the third quarter of the entire series.

8) The mother never appears in the first two groups of either half, and only once outside the last group in either half, in no. 10, the only time she is sole speaker. She does not speak in the second half.

9) An unidentified voice speaks in the last poem of the first half and the first poem of the second half.

## 2. The Sequence of Genres

The overall sequence of genres is subject to several constraints:

1) Every Invitation is followed immediately by a Renunciation, except in the case of no. 31, where a sequence of two Invitations is followed by a sequence of two Renunciations, to mark the end of the series.

2) Every Invitation (except of course no. 1) is preceded by one or more texts in which the girl's affective disposition is vacillating and/or she is being addressed in Komoi spoken by the boy or on his behalf by some other person.

3) Every Renunciation by the girl (except nos. 31-32) is followed either by a Vacillation or a Komos.

4) The microsequences (beginning with the first poem after a Renunciation and ending with the next Renunciation) increase in length (number of texts) until the last microsequence:

| Microsequence | Cantigas | Length |
|---|---|---|
| First | (1-2) | 2 |
| Second | (3-5) | 3 |
| Third | (6-9) | 4 |
| Fourth | (10-14) | 5 |
| Fifth | (15-20) | 6 |
| Sixth | (21-27) | 7 |
| Seventh | (28-32) | 5 |

The last microsequence is exceptional because it moves from a Renunciation in no. 27, through one Vacillation (no. 28) and immediately into a double Invitation, followed by a double Renunciation. If we consider these two pairs (29-30 and 31-32) as single units, we see that the final microsequence consists of **V I R**, which I shall call the basic kernel sequence (i.e., the dialectical pair **I-R** augmented by **V**). The complete sequence of genres may thus be represented as follows:[2]

First    **I**       **R**

| Second | V | I | R | | | | |
|---|---|---|---|---|---|---|---|
| Third | K | V | I | R | | | |
| Fourth | K | V | K | I | R | | |
| Fifth | R(V) | R/K | W | P | K | R | |
| Sixth | K/V | R/K | K | S/P | V/K | I | R |
| Seventh | V | I | I | R | R | | |

The following observations are made on the basis of this analysis:
1) The first microsequence represents the minimum sequence, or rather contains representatives of the two principal genres of the girl's discourse, **I** and **R**.
2) Each microsequence after the first contains at least one **V**.
3) Between the second and the fourth microsequences this kernel is expanded from **V I R** to **K V I R** to **K V K I R**, that is, a Komos is inserted before the **V** in the third microsequence, and before both the **V** and the **I** in the fourth microsequence.
4) The fifth and sixth microsequences are the longest, and display the greatest variety of genres. The fifth begins with two texts in which the direction of the sequence of functions is renunciatory (one of these is a dialog in which the other voice is komastic) and also contains a narrative text in which the speaker is an unidentified persona (no. 17), and a Propemptikon. The sixth microsequence contains five dialogs, four of them between boy and girl (the only such in the series, discounting the mysterious no. 16), as well as the most generically complex poem in the series (no. 24).
5) The seventh microsequence marks a return to the basic kernel, but with an expansion of **I** and **R** to two poems each.
6) Each microsequence ends with a Renunciation by the girl.

## 3. The Affective Disposition of the Girl

The girl's affective disposition in the first half of the series shows the following pattern:

| + | – | –+ | + | – | (K) | –+ | + |
|---|---|---|---|---|---|---|---|
| 1 | 2 | 3 | 4 | 5 | 6 | 7 | 8 |

| – | (K) | –+ | (K) | + | – | –+ | –/(K) |
|---|---|---|---|---|---|---|---|
| 9 | 10 | 11 | 12 | 13 | 14 | 15 | 16 |

Discounting the Komoi (except in the case of no. 16, in which she speaks), the pattern of her affective disposition is constant until the last poem of the first half, repeating the sequence +, –, –+. This pattern is interrupted at no. 16, so that it forms the sequence +, –, –+, – with which the first half ends. This break in the pattern is caused by the fact that in no. 16 the direction of the sequence of functions is renunciatory. The presence of a Renunciation at this structurally privileged position is a clear indication of the importance of the Renunciation in the structuring of the series, and signals the renunciatory direction of the sequence of genres in the entire series.

In the second half (17-32) the pattern of the girl's affective disposition is as follows:

| + | + | (K) | – | –+ | – | (K) | + |
|---|---|-----|---|----|---|-----|---|
| 17 | 18 | 19 | 20 | 21 | 22 | 23 | 24 |

| –+ | + | – | –+ | + | + | – | – |
|----|---|---|----|---|---|---|---|
| 25 | 26 | 27 | 28 | 29 | 30 | 31 | 32 |

We have seen, in the commentary on no. 26, that between no. 19 and no. 26 the pattern is perfectly symmetrical. This symmetrical section is preceded by two +'s, and followed by a Renunciation (–), which, in its turn, is followed by the basic kernel sequence, represented in generic terms by **V I R**, and in terms of affective disposition by –+, +, –.

Both halves of the series display remarkable symmetries in the pattern of the girl's affective disposition. The sequence of texts which overlaps the juncture of the two halves (forming a kind of generic stretto relative to the halves) displays the pattern:

| – | –+ | –(K) | + | + |
|---|----|------|---|---|
| 14 | 15 | 16 | 17 | 18 |

This sequence (analyzed here as a series of five texts, since we are dealing with patterns of affective disposition and not of genre, as above), displays the basic kernel sequence we have seen repeated three times previously in the first half (–, –+, +) with the interpolation of a second – (in no. 16) and the doubling of the + (at a crucial point in the story: the two +'s represent the "Washing" poem and the post-rendezvous Propemptikon).

## 4. The Symmetries of Generic Forms and Affective Dispositions Seen in the Division of Texts into Groups of Four, Eight, and Sixteen

The distributions of genres in the first half can be schematized as follows:

|   |   |   |     |
|---|---|---|-----|
| I | R | R | I   |
| R | K | K | R   |
| V | V | V | R   |
| I | I | K | R/K |

The patterns here are as follows:

1) In the first position:       **I**         **R**         **R**         **I**
2) In the second position:    **R**         **K**         **K**         **R**
3) In the third position:     **V**         **V**         **V**      **R(V)**
4) **I** is in the fourth position in the first two groups, and **K** is in fourth position in the third and fourth groups, sharing the position with **R** in the final poem of the first half ("ay flores"). It should be noted that the so-called Komos in the last position in the third group is the "Other Woman" poem. Its location in a privileged position may be regarded as a prefiguring of the infidelity we have detected in no. 31.

The affective dispositions which correspond to these genres are as follows:

|      |      |         |          |
|------|------|---------|----------|
| +    | –    | –       | +        |
| –    | –    | –       | –        |
| –+   | –+   | –+      | –+       |
| +    | +    | (K)     | –(K)     |

The – in the last position in the fourth group is diametrically opposed to the + in the first position of the first group, but in harmony with the – in the last position in the last group in the second half (no. 32).

The distribution of genres by groups in the second half is as follows:[3]

|   |     |     |   |
|---|-----|-----|---|
| W | K/V | K/V | I |
| P | R/K | I/K | I |
| K | K   | R   | R |
| R | S/P | V   | R |

As I have noted above, the variety of genres in the second half is much greater than that in the first half. Leaving aside the mysterious no. 17, we have a Propemptikon (no. 18), a Syntaktikon-Renunciation/Schetliastic Propemptikon (no. 24), and four other dialogs, though in no. 24 the girl speaks only four verses, and in no. 26 the boy speaks only two. We may note that with the exception of no. 24, which marks the 3/4 point in the overall series, the other four dialogs in the second half occur in the first and second positions of the sixth and seventh (that is, the inner) groups. One half of each of these four dialogs is komastic. The girl's half is vacillatory in the dialogs in the first position, and renunciatory or "inviting" in the dialogs in the second position. The third position shows the pattern (across the groups) **K K R R**. In the first and second positions in the outer two groups (five and eight) the girl's attitude, whether implicit (in the case of the fifth group) or explicit (in the last group) is positive.

The girl's affective disposition in the texts in the second half is as follows:

```
 +        -+        -+        +
 +        -         +         +
                    -         -
 -        +         -+        -
```

The linear pattern in this sequence is more obviously symmetrical than the pattern seen in the groups of four. But we may note that the cardinal positions (first and last positions in the fifth and eighth groups) are occupied in each case by + in the first position and − in the last, and that the second position in each of the two outer groups is also occupied by a +. The first and last positions in the inner two groups are occupied in every case but one by −+; and if we look closely at that exception, we shall see that it occurs in a text which occupies the 3/4 mark in the overall series, no. 24, which is primarily a discourse by the boy, and in which the girl's positive reaction marks a transition from her negative disposition in the two preceding texts towards her positive disposition in no. 26.

The third position is nowhere occupied in the second half by a text which shows a positive affective disposition on the part of the girl. In groups five and six (nos. 19 and 23) she is being informed (by a friend) of the boy's amorous suffering and is not moved to pity, in groups seven and eight (nos. 27 and 31) she utters Renunciations. Curiously, although the second half is dominated by the boy's komastic activity and the girl's rejection of him, three of the four texts in the second position show a clearly positive affective disposition. If we supply an affective disposition in the texts where the girl is being wooed (in one way or another) and consider that this disposition is negative (since she does not relent), the pattern becomes:

```
 +        -+        -+        +
 +        -         +         +
 -        -         -         -
 -        +         -+        -
```

The only positions which are not rigorously symmetrical are no. 24, at the 3/4 mark, and no. 26, the Invitation which crowns the komastic activities of nos. 19-25. These two texts, asymmetrical with respect to this chart, are structurally privileged on two other (and distinct) levels of analysis: no. 24 in the analysis of quarter units; no. 26 in the analysis of generic microsequences (cf. above, pp. 91-92).

I have dealt above with the symmetries shown by the breakdown of the series into groups of four. A breakdown into groups of eight shows that the texts which occupy the positions at the end of each quarter exhibit the following pattern:

| I | R/K | S(R)/P | R |
|---|-----|--------|---|
| 8 | 16  | 24     | 32 |

The girl's discourses at the end of the first half and at the three quarter mark are Renunciation and Propemptikon, respectively. The schetliasmos shows a positive affective disposition. The pattern of her affective dispositions in the texts marking the end of each of the four quarter units of the series is therefore:

+          –          +          –

The outer two texts in this pattern of four are spoken solely by the girl and are an Invitation and a Renunciation, respectively. The inner two texts consist of complex discourses: in the first case (no. 16) a dialog in which the girl's Renunciation contains an ambiguous sequence of topoi in the first two stanzas and the response is a Komos uttered by an unidentified voice; in the second case a renunciatory Syntaktikon with a komastic motive whose countergenre (the girl's discourse) is (the schetliasmos of) a Propemptikon. This latter text is the only one in the entire series of 32 in which the boy dominates (6 of 7 vv. in the stanza, 2 of 3 in the *fiinda*), and, even if komastic from the point of view of motive, is a Renunciation from the point of view of genre. If we consider the girl's reply an Invitation— it is an implicit invitation to remain—we have the following pattern:

|                  | 1/4 | 2/4 | 3/4 | 4/4 |
|------------------|-----|-----|-----|-----|
| Girl's discourse | I   | R   | I   | R   |
| Boy's discourse  |     | K   | R   |     |

The symmetries here are as follows:
1) The girl's discourses follow the pattern **I R I R**
2) In the inner two texts in the pattern, the girl utters a Renunciation which is answered by a Komos, and then an Invitation in response to a Renunciation.
3) The boy's discourse is represented only in the inner two texts in the pattern.
   a) In the first case this discourse is a Komos spoken by an unidentified voice;
   b) In the second case this discourse is a Renunciation spoken by the boy.
4) After the girl's Invitation at the end of the first quarter of the series, each of the texts marking the end of the subsequent quarters contains a Renunciation, first by the girl, then by the boy, then by the girl.
5) The only discourse actually spoken by the boy at a position marking the end of the quarter is a Renunciation occurring at the three quarter mark, and is, generically, the most complex text in the series. It is the only Renunciation in the entire series spoken by the boy.
6) Both halves end with Renunciations.
7) At the end of the first half the Renunciation is answered by a Komos.
8) At the end of the second half the Renunciation is unanswered.

## 5. Fiinda

It has been demonstrated that this series of 32 *cantigas d'amigo* shows clear patterns on several different levels of analysis. The patterns revealed by these four aspects of the text are not a matter of subjective interpretation. The identification of genres is occasionally problematic (e.g., no. 17, which we have been content to call "Washing"), but the identifications made here are based on the analysis of sequences of topoi, a subject which has been dealt with in detail in Chapter One and for which the theoretical foundations have been established on an empirical basis. The assessment of the girl's affective dispositions has been made in every case on the basis of a detailed analysis of topoi, lexical elements and dramatic situation, and has been corroborated whenever possible by reference to other texts in this series. The patterns in the distribution of personae as speaker and addressee are objective facts, derived in every case from textual evidence. (In the two texts, nos. 16 and 17, where it was not possible to identify a speaker, I have referred to this speaker as an unidentified voice.) The patterns clearly exist, and are evidence that this series of texts has been ordered according to a complex logic.

If we agree that this set of 32 *cantigas d'amigo* has been carefully ordered according to several criteria, the question arises: Who ordered the text? There are two possible answers: the poet or someone else. This someone else could be a contemporary of the poet who was given the task of selecting and ordering a group of *cantigas* (it should be remembered that the poet, as King of Portugal, could easily have availed himself of the services of a scribe or a scholar), or it could be any other individual who, having access to the *cancioneiro* of Dom Dinis, decided or was asked to impose some order on a random set of texts. At any rate, the texts appear in this order in both of the *cancioneiros* in which they are found. Since the Italian apographs appear to be copies of a *cancioneiro* from Portugal or Spain, it would appear certain that even if the texts were not ordered by the poet they were ordered by someone who must surely have been familiar with the poetics of the medieval Galego-Portuguese lyric. It is my belief that the texts were ordered by the poet himself. Since poets organize groups of syllables into verses, groups of verses into stanzas and groups of stanzas into poems, it is reasonable to suppose that they should want to and be able to organize groups of poems into cycles. We have at least two clear and undisputed examples of an organized cycle of poems in the Galego-Portuguese love lyric: the seven *cantigas* of Martim Codax and the nine *cantigas* of Pero Meogo. Other editors of individual *cancioneiros* by Galego-Portuguese poets have tried to demonstrate the existence of cycles.[4] Their results have not always been convincing, and it is by no means to be supposed that all *cancioneiros* contain cycles of *cantigas*. The 20 *cantigas d'amigo* of Dom Dinis which follow our set of 32 in the *cancioneiros* do not, in my opinion, contain a cycle, although some of the texts do seem linked. In his *cantigas d'amor*, the preponderance of Komoi (about 58 of them) seems to rule out any sense of a logical development. Neither the fact that the individual *cancioneiros* of other poets in the corpus do not contain cycles, nor the fact that neither the other *cantigas d'amigo* of Dom Dinis nor his *cantigas d'amor* seem to contain cycles precludes, however, the possibility that this set of 32 does. Each set of texts must be judged on the evidence provided by the texts themselves.

Another question is whether the poet, assuming he ordered the poems, set out to compose a series of 32 *cantigas d'amigo* telling a single story, or whether he wrote the texts first and then ordered them to present the appearance of a coherent sequence. This question cannot be answered with certainty, nor does it affect our analysis of the series. The poems are ordered; and just as there is no reason to think that the poet did not order them, there is no reason to think that he did not write them as a set.

A third question which presents itself is whether we should assume that the girl is the same girl in all 32 *cantigas*. There is nothing in any of the 32 texts which rules out the possibility of a story involving one girl, one boy, a mother and a friend. (The friend, of course, need not always be the same, though her discourses and her attitudes would seem to indicate that she is always partial to the boy, describing his suffering, defending him, delivering his messages and arguing his case.) But, even if neither the girl nor any of the personae were the same in any two of the 32 texts, they would still constitute a series in which each text represents a successive stage in the development of a generalized love story, and in which the personae could never be distinguished from their counterparts in the other texts—which would amount to the same thing as a series of texts in which the personae were always the same.

The writing of the story of love in a sequence of poetic texts is what I call erotic mythography: the *graphia* (writing) of the *mythos* (story) of *eros* (love). I would argue that in these 32 *cantigas*, the poet, Dom Dinis, has assumed the responsibility of producing an elaborate version of what may safely be called the Galego-Portuguese poem-cycle. (Tavani is careful not to try to define the nature of this concept too narrowly.[5]) Within this erotic mythography the Renunciation has been shown to be important from a purely structural point of view:

1) Each successive microsequence is capped by a Renunciation and the renunciatory direction of the sequence of functions is clearer with each successive Renunciation.
2) Each of the last three quarters of the series ends with a Renunciation.
3) The first half ends with a sequence of three Renunciations, the second half with a sequence of two Renunciations

The generic dialectic is dynamic in this series. The girl's Renunciation is opposed to her Invitation and always follows it. Her Renunciation is also opposed to the boy's Komos, and all examples of Komoi (spoken by him or anyone else on his behalf) occur somewhere between Renunciations (by the girl) and Invitations. His Komos never follows an Invitation. Moreover, the girl's persistent renunciatory attitude in the seventh microsequence is met in no. 24 by a Renunciation delivered by the boy, which is the key to his successful komastic strategy in that microsequence. From the point of view of generic analysis, the entire series is based on these oppositions, whose dialectical tensions sustain the dynamics of the set. It is extremely significant that each time **K** is momentarily greeted by **I** (i.e., in every Invitation) the tension in the series is immediately renewed by a Renunciation.

\* \* \* \* \*

In this study I have purposely avoided any mention of several contexts, historical and literary, in which the corpus of Dom Dinis is located. Ringed by the rest of the Galego-Portuguese lyric—which it nevertheless dominates numerically (52 of c. 504 *cantigas d'amigo*, 75 of c. 725 *cantigas d'amor*)—the poetry of Dom Dinis, like that of the entire "school," is situated within at least two different traditions, which we may call for convenience the male and female discourses (and which are associated with Provençal lyric and the Kharjas, respectively[6]). The corpus of medieval love lyric, in Latin, Provençal, Portuguese, Italian, French, Spanish, Catalan, German and English, stands in relation, synchronically, with a still wider context, including Sanskrit and Arabic (whether or not there is any direct influence in either direction), and, historically, in the context of both classical poetry—Greek, Latin, Hebrew, Arabic, etc.—and the so called Renaissance love-lyric, which surely grew out of it. (We can see Renaissance poetics clearly enough in some of the Provençal *trobadors*, or for that matter, in the poetry of Dom Dinis).

It would be unwise to suppose that great historical movements (the invasion of the Iberian Peninsula by the Moors in the eighth century, the movements of Germanic and other tribes) and ancient cultural institutions (matriarchy, for instance) are not somehow reflected in the poetry of the Galego-Portuguese school, or that there is no connection between medieval Romance love lyric especially and classical Latin (or for that matter Greek) poetry.

Even the poetics of so limited an area as Western Europe represents a vast challenge to history and philology. The poetic, however, is not merely a historical phenomenon, but also one with a certain ontological independence.

Thus, without denying the all too obvious relation of Dom Dinis to the Galego-Portuguese school, or of that school to the Provençal and French lyric, and probably also to a wide-spread "school" of feminine-voiced lyric which seems to have existed all across Europe as early as the eleventh century and possibly much earlier,—without denying these relations, or the relation of this lyric to traces of feminine-voiced lyric in Latin and Greek poetry (to stay within the confines of Europe)—affirming, that is, the value of historical and sociological studies, philological studies, musical studies, semiotics, and the like, I have nevertheless chosen as the object of my comparative study a single corpus of thirty-two poems, product of a slender muse that flourished in the thirteenth century in Portugal. But though the muse be slender, the strophic construction is robust: thirty-two *cantigas* bound in a precise configuration of sets of eight, inscribed by a series of patterned generic microsequences, whose modulations and cadences articulate, along a syntagmatic axis, a (vertical) harmonic structure whose tonic is the Renunciation.

# Notes

## Notes to the Introduction

[1] Hans Robert Jauss, "Theory of Genres and Medieval Literature," In *Toward an Aesthetic of Reception*, Timothy Bahti, trans. (Minneapolis: University of Minnesota Press, 1982), pp. 76-109. This article originally appeared in the series *Grundriss der Romanischen Literaturen des Mittelalters*, VI (Heidelberg: Carl Winter, Universitätsverlag, 1972).

[2] This is the complaint voiced by Vladimir Propp, in the first chapter of the *Morphology of the Folktale*, (1928). Jean-Marie D'Heur, in *Recherches internes sur la lyrique amoureuse des troubadours galiciens-portugais* (XIIᵉ-XIVᵉ siècles) (Liège: Publications de la Faculté de Philosophie et Lettres de l'Université de Liège, 1975), has made a start, and his data must be taken into account in any classification which seeks to clarify the problem of genre. This study is not, of course, a morphology of the *cantiga d'amigo*, nor even of the genre which I shall be calling Renunciation, as that genre is evidenced in the corpus of (about) 500 *cantigas d'amigo* in the Galego-Portuguese lyric. It is a typology of the texts in a corpus of 32 *cantigas d'amigo* of Dom Dinis which I take to be a sequence (of discourses) constituting the story of a renunciation. Perhaps some will argue that even if this sequence was intended as a complete "cycle" of poems, it would constitute the story of a love affair. My point, then, is that this love affair is structured as a renunciation. The existence of the "genre" of Renunciation in Galego-Portuguese lyric has never been posited, as far as I know, though some editors have discussed the importance of individual Renunciations without conceding this type of discourse status as a "genre" or even as a sub-genre. This is partly due to the prevailing conception of what constitutes a genre in medieval Galego-Portuguese love lyric. By my count, there are at least 34 explicit Renunciations among the *cantigas d'amigo* (not including those by Dom Dinis).

In the following list the first number is that assigned to the text in José Joaquim Nunes, ed., *Cantigas d'amigo dos trovadores galego-portugueses*, 3 vols. (Coimbra: Imprensa da Universidade, 1926-1928)—converted, however, into arabic numerals— and the numbers in parentheses refer to the numeration of the codices (V= Cod. 4803, Biblioteca Vaticana; B= Cod. 10991, Biblioteca Nacional, Lisboa, also called the Canzoniere Colocci-Brancuti; for both, see the bibliography under Cintra, Monaci, Molteni, Braga, Machado). The names of the poets are cited not from Nunes, but directly from the list of poets in the "Tavola Colocciana, Autori Portughesi," Ed. Elsa Gonçalves, *Arquivos do Centro Cultural Português*, X (1976), 387-448. (Where the attribution in the *Tavola* is at variance with that in the manuscripts, I have given the latter, spelling the name as it is given in B.)

| 74  | (V 241, B 640)     | [?]Pae Soarez                         |
|-----|--------------------|----------------------------------------|
| 84  | (V 251, B 650)     | Pero Garcia Burgales                   |
| 103 | (V 271, B 668)     | Dom Joham d'Avoyn                       |
| 105 | (V 273, B 670)     | "           "                          |
| 108 | (V 276, B 674)     | "           "                          |
| 110 | (V 278, B 676)     | "           "                          |
| 111 | (V 280, B 678)     | Don Joham Soarez Coelho                |
| 128 | (V 297, B 696)     | Joham Lopez d'Ulhoa                     |
| 147 | (V 314, B 713)     | Roy Queymado                           |
| 164 | (V 330, B 729)     | Affonso Meendez de Beesteyros          |
| 170 | (V 337, B 736)     | Pero Vyvyaez                           |
| 190 | (V 358, B 755)     | Joham de Guilhade                      |
| 192 | (V 360, B 777)     | "           "                          |
| 194 | (V 369, B 785)     | "           "                          |
| 196 | (V 371, B 787)     | "           "                          |
| 216 | (V 388, B 804)     | Fernan Froyaz                          |
| 226 | (V 403, B 819)     | Fernan Velho                           |
| 237 | (V 416, B 830)     | Pedr'Anes Solaz                        |
| 239 | (V 418, B 832)     | Pero da Ponte                          |
| 268 | (V 517, B 929)     | Roy Fernandez clerigo                  |
| 270 | (V 519, B 931)     | "           "                          |
| 275 | (V 525, B 937)     | Sancho Sanchez clerigo                 |
| 285 | (V 598)            | Joham Ayras, burg[u]es de Santiago     |
| 325 | (V 641, B 1051)    | "           "                          |
| 345 | (V 710, B 1119)    | Pero de Berdia                         |
| 346 | (V 711, B 1120)    | "           "                          |
| 347 | (V 712, B 1120bis) | "           "                          |
| 399 | (V 776, B 1170)    | Juião Bo[l]sseyro                      |
| 442 | (V 834, B 1229)    | Joham Baveca                           |
| 447 | (V 839, B 1234)    | "           "                          |
| 451 | (V 843, B 1238)    | Martin Padrozelos                      |
| 463 | (V 856, B 1251)    | Lopo jograr                            |
| 470 | (V 863, B 1258)    | Galisteu Fernandiz                     |
| 481 | (V 874, B 1268)    | Joham de Canga[s]                      |

In all of the above texts, there are explicit examples of the topos which in this study is called the renunciation proper. A morphology of the Renunciation in the *cantigas d'amigo* would also have to take into account many other texts which document the lexicon of the Renunciation, recount, refer to, or imply renunciations. Even discounting many texts in which anger, perjury, indiscretion, infidelity, etc. are mentioned without an explicit renunciation, the following poems should, I think, be taken into account:

| 75  | (V 242, B 641)  | Nuno Fernandez Torneol    |
|-----|-----------------|---------------------------|
| 83  | (V 250, B 649)  | Pero Garcia Burgales      |
| 92  | (V 259, B 658)  | Ayras Carpancho           |
| 116 | (V 285, B 683)  | Don Joham Soarez Coelho    |
| 130 | (V 299, B 698)  | Joam Lopez d'Ulhoa        |
| 131 | (V 300, B 699)  | "            "            |
| 132 | (V 301, B 700)  | "            "            |
| 134 | (V 303, B 702)  | Don Fernandez Cogominho   |
| 141 | (V 310, B 709)  | Gonçal' Eanes de Vinhal   |
| 142 | (V 311, B 710)  | "            "            |
| 172 | (V 339, B 738)  | Don Affonso Lopez de Bayam |
| 267 | (V 516, B 928)  | Roy Fernandez clerigo     |
| 277 | (V 527, B 939)  | Sancho Sanchez clerigo    |
| 339 | (V 822, B 1217) | Pedr' Amigo de Sevilha    |
| 352 | (V 722, B 1130) | Pero de Veer              |
| 424 | (V 802, B 1197) | Martin de Caldas          |
| 428 | (V 806, B 1201) | Nuno Treez                |
| 436 | (V 828, B 1223) | Joham Baveca              |
| 453 | (V 845, B 1240) | Martin Padrozelos         |

But this list includes only a few of the many texts which may be implicit Renunciations or partake of the thematic and lexical modalities of the genre.

[3]Giuseppe Tavani, "La poesia lirica galego-portoghese," in *Les Genres lyriques*, Vol. II, Tome I, fascicule 6, *Grundriss der Romanischen literaturen des Mittelalters*, Erich Kohler, ed. (Heidelberg: Carl Winter, Universitätsverlag, 1980), pp. 61-128. The *alba* and *pastorela* are treated as "generi contaminati" by Tavani (pp. 138-146). For the *alba*, cf. Giuseppe Tavani, "Motivi della canzone d'alba in una cantiga di Nuno Fernandez Torneol," *Annali del Istituto Universitario Orientale di Napoli—Sezione Romanza*, III, 1 (1961), 199-205, rpt. in _____, *Poesia del Duecento nella Penisola Iberica*. *Problemi della lirica galego-portoghese*, Officina Romanica, collana diretta da Aurelio Roncaglia, 12; Sezione di studi e testi portoghesi e brasiliani a cura di Luciana Stegagno Picchio, 7 (Roma: Edizioni dell'Ateneo, 1969), pp. 265-274. For the *pastorela* in Dom Dinis, see especially Luciana Stegagno Picchio, "Filtri d'oggi per testi medievali: 'Hū papagay muy fremoso'," *Arquivos do Centro Cultural Português, Homenagem a Marcel Bataillon*, 12 (1975), pp. 3-41; rpt. in _____, *A lição do texto. Filologia e literatura. I-Idade Media* (Lisboa: Edições 70, 1979), pp. 27-66; and again in _____, *La Méthode philologique* (Paris: Fundação Calouste Gulbenkian-Centro Cultural Português, 1982), pp. 7-45. The standard classifications are repeated in Frede Jensen, *The Earliest Portuguese Lyrics* (Odense: Odense University Press, 1978) pp. 41-143.

[4]For a description of this "iambic" (i.e. invective) verse, see Tavani, "La poesia lirica," pp. 109-128. For the text, of course, Manuel Rodrigues Lapa, ed., *Cantigas d'escarnho e de mal dizer dos cancioneiros medievais galego-portugueses*, 2nd ed.

(Vigo: Editorial Galaxia, 1970).

[5]For the text of the fragmentary *poetica*, see Jean-Marie D'Heur, "L' 'Art de trouver' du Chansonnier Colocci-Brancuti, Édition et analyse," *Arquivos do Centro Cultural Português*, IX (1975), 321-398.

[6]"And since there are some *cantigas* in which they [masc.] and they [fem.] speak as well, it is therefore good that you understand if they are [*cantigas*] *d'amor*, [or] if [they are *cantigas*] *d'amigo*; for [you should] know that, if they [masc.] speak in the first *cobra*, and they [fem.] in the next [lit. other], [it is a *cantiga*] *d'amor*, since the discourse [*rrazõ*] proceeds [lit. "moves"] from him, as we told you before. And if they [fem.] speak in the first *cobra*, it is therefore [a *cantiga*] *d'amigo*. And if both speak in one *cobra*, it is therefore [to be classified] according to which of them speaks first in the *cobra*."

[7]As Nunes (*Cantigas d'amigo*, Vol. I, p. 2) points out, the distinction "não era tão rigorosa que não deixasse de ser transgredida, pelo menos na cantiga no. XXIV desta colecção," which is precisely no. 21 in the corpus presented in this study. In Giuseppe Tavani, *Repertorio metrico della lirica galego-portoghese*, Officina Romanica, collana diretta da Aurelio Roncaglia, 7, Sezione di studi e testi portoghesi e brasiliani a cura di Luciana Stegagno Picchio, 5 (Roma: Edizioni dell'Ateneo, 1967), p. 395, as well as in Jean-Marie D'Heur, "Nomenclature des Troubadours Galiciens-Portugais (XIIe-XIVe siècles), Table de concordance de leurs chansonniers, et liste des incipit de leurs compositions," *Arquivos do Centro Cultural Português*, VII (1973), 17-100, this *cantiga* is classified as a *cantiga d'amor* despite its location in the manuscripts among the *cantigas d'amigo* of Dom Dinis. As I shall show, this text, whatever we choose to call it, belongs precisely where it is found. Silvio Pellegrini, *Studi su trove e trovatori della prima lirica ispano-portoghese*, 2a. ed. riveduta e aumentata, Biblioteca di filologia romanza diretta da Giuseppe E. Sansone, 3 (Bari: Adriatica Editrice, 1959), to support his assertion that the "struttura piuttosto caotica di quei manoscritti" precludes even the formulation of the hypothesis that the poems of Dom Dinis are found in some kind of original order, points out the *pastorelas*— which he would attach to the *cantigas d'amigo*—are found among the *cantigas d'amor*, that various *cantigas d'amigo* (our nos. 21, 24, 25, 26) are written "in stile aulico" and that one *cantiga d'amigo* (our no. 17) ". . . non può propriamente chiamarsi *d'amigo*, e si presenta invece come un tema narrativo d'un certo sapore umoristico," pp. 165-168. Rather than preempting further study of the problem, his observations should have provoked two questions: 1) Why should we prefer the testimony of the *poetica* in B— whose authorship and date are uncertain (cf. note 5) — to the evidence of the texts themselves? 2) Given the possibility —however remote— that those texts serve a function within an organized sequence, should we not examine the entire corpus of Dom Dinis carefully to see if such a sequence exists? Tavani, "La poesia lirica," pp. 40-41, is content, however, to repeat (i.e. cite) Pellegrini's assertion.

[8]Tavani, "La poesia lirica," pp. 61-83. The existence of a poetic genre of Renunciation in classical Greek and Roman poetry has been demonstrated beyond

a doubt by Francis Cairns, first in *Generic Composition in Greek and Roman Poetry* (Edinburgh: Edinburgh University Press, 1972) pp. 79-82, and then in "Self-Imitation within a Generic Framework: Ovid *Amores* 2.9 and 3.11 and the *Renuntiatio Amoris*," in *Creative Imitation and Latin Literature*, David West and Tony Woodman, eds. (Cambridge: Cambridge University Press, 1979). pp. 121-141. The only full length study I know of concerning the Renunciation (other than Ovid's *Remedia Amoris*, which is a handbook for renouncers) is to be found in Louis B. Salomon, *The Devil Take Her! A Study of the Rebellious Lover in English Poetry* (Philadelphia: University of Pennsylvania Press, 1931; rpt., New York: A.S. Barnes and Company, Inc., 1961), which has an excellent bibliography of Renunciations in English (pp. 300-351). Salomon omits, however, both the Renunciations in Shakespeare's sonnets (most of nos. 127-154, and several to the "boy") and all of the examples in Chaucer (including the "Compleynt of Anelida the Quene upon fals Arcite," a *cantiga d'amigo* parading as a gigantic *canzone*, whose sequence of functions, marked by patterned modulations, has a renunciatory cadential function). My article, "The 'Renuntiatio Amoris' in 'Canção X'," in *Quaderni Portoghesi* 7-8 (Primavera Autunno 1980), 169-198, though centered on a text of Camões, suggests that the Renunciation deserves wider study and that the traditional thematics of the genre have generated some of the western tradition's best poems.

[9]The Komos is technically a genre of Greek and Latin love poetry, and has been described by Cairns, *Generic Composition* (see the index there). I have adapted the word for the study of later love poetry (Cohen, pp. 169-198) to try to displace some of the prejudicial terminology, such as "courtly love poetry," etc.

[10]Tavani, "La poesia lirica," p. 61, says that this type of lyric composition is "[s]trutturato, tranne poche eccezioni, come richiesta d'amore del poeta alla dama o come lamento per l'indifferenza e l'altera distanza di lei. . ." Where absent, the request is usually implied.

[11]This diversity, freely admitted by modern editors, is directly related to the question of poem cycles and sequences. See Friederich Diez, *Ueber die erste portugiesische Kunst-und Hofpoesie* (Bonn: E. Weber, 1863), pp. 97-98; Alfred Jeanroy, *Les Origines de la poésie lyrique en France au moyen âge*, 3e ed. (Paris: Librarie Ancienne Honoré Champion, 1925), p. 315; Henry R. Lang, *Das Liederbuch des Königs Denis von Portugal* (Halle A. S.: Max Niemeyer, 1894 rpt. Hildesheim, New York: Georg Olms Verlag, 1972), p. LXIV; Nunes, *Cantigas d'amigo*, III, p. 9; Giuseppe Tavani, "Spunti narrativi e drammatici nel Canzoniere di Joam Nunes Camanes," *Annali dell'Istituto Universitario Orientale di Napoli—Sezione Romanza*, II, 2 (1960), 47-70; _____, "Parallelismo e iterazione. Apunti in margine al criterio jakobsoniano di pertinenza," *Cultura Neolatina*, XXXIII (1973), 9-32; Leodegário A. de Azevedo Filho, ed. *As cantigas de Pero Meogo* (Rio de Janeiro: Edições Gernasa, 1974), pp. 87-101; Fernanda Toriello, ed. *Fernand'Esquyo, Le poesie*, Pubbl. dei seminari di Portoghese e Brasiliano della Facoltà di Lettere dell'Università di Roma e della Facoltà di Lingue dell'Università di Bari—Studi e Testi,1 (Bari: Adriatica Editrice, 1976), p. 58; Carmelo Zilli, ed., *Johan Baveca, Poesie*, Biblioteca di

filologia romanza diretta da Giuseppe E. Sansone, 30 (Bari: Adriatica Editrice, 1977), pp. 37-38; Giulia Lanciani, ed., *Il canzoniere di Fernan Velho*, Romanica Vulgaria— Collezione di testi medievali romanzi diretta da Giuseppe Tavani, 1 (L' Aquila, Italia: Japadre Editore, 1977), pp. 30-41; Maria Luisa Indini, ed., *Bernal de Bonval, Poesie*, Biblioteca di filologia romanza diretta da Giuseppe E. Sansone, 32 (Bari: Adriatica Editrice, 1978), pp. 67-68; Carmen M. Radulet, ed., *Estevam Fernandez d'Elvas, Il Canzoniere* (Bari: Adriatica Editrice 1979), p. 42; Ettore Finazzi-Agrò, ed., *Il canzoniere di Johan Mendiz de Briteyros*, Romanica Vulgaria —Collezione de testi medievali romanzi diretta da Giuseppe Tavani, 2 (L'Aquila: Japadre Editore, 1979), pp. 40-61; Tavani, "La poesia lirica...," pp. 55-61, 91-109. Eugenio Asensio, *Poética y realidad en el cancionero peninsular de la Edad Media*, 2nd ed. (Madrid: Gredos, 1970), speaks of "la anexión de otros géneros más particularizados por la canción de mujer, o mejor, de doncella" (p. 22).

[12]Azevedo Filho's comment (*Pero Meogo*, p. 88) "na verdade, a cantiga de amigo é produto de uma intersecção de gêneros, numa fase ainda primitiva de gestação de formas," is only apparently similar to my own here. By "genres" he means "narrative" and "dramatic," as is clear in context. A more important distinction is that I am suggesting that the *cantiga d'amigo* is the location of a complex of genres at a late period in the development of the medieval peninsular *cantiga*.

[13]Cairns, *Generic Composition*, pp. 6-7, but the treatment (by Greek and Latin poets) of primary and secondary elements is discussed throughout the book.

[14]Cairns, *Generic Composition*, pp. 177-245, discusses speaker- and addressee-variation in texts of Sappho, Theocritos, Catullus, Horace, Propertius, Tibullus, Ovid, etc.

[15]The flawed numeration of the *cantigas d'amor* can be seen at a glance in the list of Pellegrini, *Studi*, pp. 175-178 or in that of D'Heur, "Nomenclature." Dom Dinis's love poetry has been edited separately by Caetano Lopes de Moura, *Cancioneiro d'el Rei D. Diniz, pela primeira vez impresso* (Paris: J.P. Aillaud, 1847) and Lang, *Das Liederbuch*, as well as in the editions of V by: Ernesto Monaci, ed., *Il canzoniere portoghese della Biblioteca Vaticana* (Halle a.S.: Max Niemeyer, 1875); Theóphilo Braga, ed., *Cancioneiro portuguez da Vaticana. Edição crítica* (Lisboa: Imprensa Nacional, 1878); and in that of B: Elsa Paxeco Machado and José Pedro Machado, eds., *Cancioneiro da Biblioteca Nacional (Colocci-Brancuti)*, 8 vols. (Lisboa: Ed. da Revista do Portugal, 1949-1964); and by Nunes in *Cantigas d'Amigo* (note 2, above) and *Cantigas d'Amor dos trovadores galego-portugueses* (Coimbra: Imprensa da Universidade, 1932). The poems appear in both manuscripsts (B and V) in the order indicated, with the last (that is, the fifty-second) *cantiga d'amigo* being followed by yet another *cantiga d'amor*, preceded by the word "Senhora," indicating that there is a change of persona, and that a male speaker will now address a female addressee. It should be noted that in both manuscripts one of the *cantigas d'amigo* appears in a fragmentary version found among the *cantigas d'amor*. See note 36 (Chapter Two) on no. 19.

[16]The attribution of this *cantiga* to Dom Dinis has been disputed by Tavani,

"Sull'attribuzione a D. Denis di *Pero muito amo, muito non desejo*," *Poesia del Duecento*, pp. 219-233.

[17]That is, following 75 *cantigas d'amor* (or 76, if we count the first version of no. 19 =V 116, B 523 bis), the first *cantiga d'amigo* is set off by the identity of the speaker, and could thus have been distinguished immediately from what precedes, even if there had been no rubric in the manuscript tradition; but the rubric makes the problem much easier. Although there is a slight difference between the two rubrics they both inform us that "From this page on begin the *cantigas d'amigo* which the very noble ['respectable' in V] Dom Dinis, King of Portugal, made." For the text of this rubric see Lang, *Das Liederbuch*, p. 66; Nunes, *Cantigas d'amigo*, III, p. 442; Machado, III, pp. 164-165.

[18]That text (B 585=V 188) is spoken by a married woman, the only such persona in the corpus of Dom Dinis—and in the entire Galego-Portuguese lyric. Although the juxtaposition may be fortuitous (cf. Chapter Two, note 45), it is also possible that this shift in persona is an indication that a series has ended on the previous text. A similar technique is used in Shapespeare's Sonnets: in 126, the last poem to the "boy," he is called "my lovely boy" in the first verse; in 127, the first sonnet addressed to the so-called "dark lady," she is referred to as "my mistress."

[19]In Chapter Three (p. 98) I shall deal briefly with the question whether the personae are constant or not.

[20]In the three pastorelas (Lang XXIII, LVII,LXX) found in the manuscripts among the *cantigas d'amor*, but presented, for instance, by Nunes among the *cantigas d'amigo*, the voice of one or more personae is quoted. See esp. Luciana Stegagno Picchio, "Filtri d'oggi." The two *cantigas d'amigo* (outside our corpus of 32, that is) in which someone other than the protagonist speaks are Lang CXVIII, CXXII.

[21]Critical text and analysis in D'Heur, "L' 'Art de Trouver'."

[22]"Lit.: *Fiindas* are [a] thing which the *trobadores* have always used to put in the ending of their *cantigas*, to conclude and end better in them the discourses ["rrazones"] which they have spoken in the *cantigas*, calling them *fiinda* because this is as much as to say, ending of discourse."

[23]The typographic distinction which I have tried to maintain in this study between "renunciation" (=any act of renunciation, as in "a long drawn out renunciation," the idea of renunciation, etc.) and "Renunciation" (=a text which can be identified as belonging to the poetic genre of Renunciation, or the genre itself) applies here. The "renunciation" mentioned in the title of this book should be lower-case. I am not arguing that the cycle, in its entirety, is a Renunciation, but that it represents the history of a renunciation, and includes, frequently and in privileged positions, Renunciations. It should perhaps be stressed that Friedrich Diez, *Ueber die erste portugiesische Kunst- und Hofpoesie*, in speaking of the *cantigas d'amigo* of Dom Dinis, suggests that "Das ganze ist ein Liebesroman, worin aber die einzelnen Gedichte nur in losem Zumsammenhange stehen" (p.97). He does not, however, think to separate the first 32 from the last 20 (no one, I believe, has thought to), and therefore feels that there is no real conclusion to the set (p. 98).

## Notes to Chapter One

[1]Tavani, "La poesia lirica," p. 64. D'Heur, *Recherches*, pp. 439-488, gives a full description of two of those topoi, "praise" and "suffering."

[2]Cairns, *Generic Composition*, esp. pp. 158-176.

[3]Lang, *Das Liederbuch*, p. 99. All texts of Dom Dinis other than those in the corpus of 32 *cantigas d'amigo* presented in Chapter Two are cited from the edition of Lang.

[4]Pellegrini, *Studi*, p. 168.

[5]Glynnis M. Cropp, *Le Vocabulaire courtois des troubadours de l'époque classique* (Genève: Librairie Droz, 1975), 226-230, and the notes there. This argument could not be made, however, for poems like Bernart de Ventadorn's famous "Can vei la lauzeta mover," where it is clearly the speaker's frustration which drives him into exile.

[6]Cf.Cohen, pp. 180, 182-183, 194-195.

[7]Cf. Lanciani, *Fernan Velho*, pp. 30-31, and Finazzi-Agrò, *Johan Mendiz de Briteyros*, pp. 43-45, 89-92; Elsa Gonçalves, *A lirica galego-portuguesa* (Lisboa: Editorial Comunicação, 1983), p. 59, who accepts my interpretation. Cohen, pp. 171, 188-189, 196, n. 14. This poem could be treated as a renunciatory Syntaktikon (see no. 24 in Chapter Two). See Cairns, *Generic Composition*, on the Syntaktikon, as well as D. A. Russell and N. G. Wilson, eds., *Menander Rhetor* (Oxford: Clarendon Press, 1981), pp. 194-201, 342-346.

[8]Cf. Ovid, *Remedia Amoris*, 629-630.

[9]Luciana Stegagno Picchio, ed., *Martin Moya, Le poesie*, Officina Romanica, collana diretta da A. Roncaglia, 11, Sezione di studi e testi portoghesi e brasiliani a cura di L. Stegagno Picchio, 6 (Roma: Edizioni dell'Ateneo 1968), p. 163, says of our passage, "il motivo dell'esilio è stravolto, provocato com'è qui quest'esilio dalla durezza della dama."

[10]Cohen, pp. 193-194.

[11]Cairns, *Generic Composition*, pp. 138-140, and _____, "Self-Imitation," 121-141.

[12]Cairns, *Generic Composition*, pp. 139-157 and _____, "Self- Imitation," 128.

[13]That is, a Renunciation in which the sequence becomes polyvalent with the second function, and ends on a function which, though normally belonging to the Komos, is nonetheless still subordinate to an overall context of renunciation.

[14]The relative clause of characteristic ("u nunca possa seer. . ." etc.) implies that the land, if he could find it, would be one such that she could never know of him nor he of her. Hence the subjunctive "possa."

## Notes to Chapter Two

N.B. My "edition" of the text was made, unfortunately, not directly from the codex [B], but from the facsimile edition with an introduction by Luís F. Lindley Cintra, *Cancioneiro da Biblioteca Nacional (Colocci-Brancuti): Cód. 10991; Reprodução Facsimilada* (Lisboa: Imprensa Nacional-Casa da Moeda, 1982).

[1]In B, "mil vezes" and "no meu coraçõ" (I 4) are on different lines, the former to the left, the latter below and to the right of it. II 4 ends with the word "vezes" and II 5 begins "cuidey ja: Que algur..." etc. For the distinction, maintained here in the analysis of topoi, between "boy's absence" and "boy's delay in returning," see Pellegrini, *Studi*, pp. 86-89, as well as notes 35 and 42 (infra), and cf. *cantigas* nos. 5, 14, 15, 16, 20, 22, 27. Clearly there exists a single macro-topos, which could be called absence, of which "delay," etc., are subdivisions. The topos, "boy's intention to return" also has its variants (see note 38). For the overtones of "alhur," cf. Indini's note (p. 110) on Bonaval's verse (in V 656, B 1065) "[que já eu. . . ] deseje de vós ben e d'alhur non" (p. 109), where it is maintained that the expression ("desejar ben d'alhur") clearly means " 'da altre persone,' cioè, 'da altre donne.' " Compare, for example, the beginning of a Renunciation by Baveca (Zilli, *Poesie*, p. 117). "Amigu', entendo que non ouvestes/ poder d'alhur viver e vēestes/ a mha mesura. . . " The euphemism is found as early as Catullus (61. 144-6): "nupta, tu quoque quae tuus/ vir petet, caue ne neges, / ni petitum *aliunde* eat" (italics mine). See also Cropp, *Le Vocabulaire*, p. 227.

[2]At II 1, the reading of B is "Tristan da se ds me valha"— which would appear to mean, "he makes himself out to be Tristan, so help me God." If this is intentional and not illusory, it would be a strange contamination. Would one then postulate the existence of a verb "tristandar" ("to go around like Tristan")?

[3]This poem is analyzed by S. Reckert, *Do Cancioneiro de Amigo*, (Lisboa: Assírio e Alvim, n.d.) pp. 219-220, but my analysis was made independently and I disagree with some of his observations—though not, of course his insistence that "a definição convencional (herdada da 'arte de trovar' que prefacia o CBN [=B]) ...está a precisar duma reformulação tipológica menos tosca."

[4]It could, of course, be argued that this text should be assigned to another genre, which could be called "request for news of the beloved," or something of the sort. The name "Invitation," is meant, however, to include subcategories such as "the request for news," "the expectation of the beloved," etc.

[5]The distinction is especially important in a poem like no. 24, which must, because of its thematic logic, be classified as a Syntaktikon or a Renunciation—or, as I shall argue, a Syntaktikon-Renunciation—even though the speaker's motive is clearly komastic.

[6]In B there is an empty line between I 1 and I 2 (which reads: "E ... Mandado" etc.) and I 2 is repeated in full. III 5 reads "Que logo mēvyaria manda." In I 1, of course, "veio" = "vejo."

[7]At II 1, B has a "z" on top of the "x." In the next verse Lang (LXXXII), Nunes (IX) and Machado (523) read "partirades." V has "pertirades" and B "ptirades" with a crossed "p". Carolina Michaëlis de Vasconcellos, "Zum Liederbuch des Königs Denis von Portugal," *Zeitschrift für Romanische Philologie*, XIX (1895), p. 528, suggests "bem lhi partira Dês [=Deus] morte."

[8]Cf. Lang, *Das Liederbuch* : "Nicht wenige unserer lieder scheinen im grunde nichts zu sein als variationen der *cantigas d'amor*, gleichsam das weibliche widerspiel dieser letztern" (p. LXXIII). Pellegrini sees stylistic unity in Dinis' handling of the two "genres" (*Studi*, pp. 167-169). See also, for example, Stegagno Picchio, "Filtri d'oggi," and Tavani, "La poesia lirica", pp. 47-58.

[9]At I 6 both V and B read "quero," with a short upward stroke over the "o"— something I have not registered in the list of changes. At I 4 V reads "cama erevo tãdo no feyto seu." Lang prints this text. Nunes, reading with B, suggests that the meaning of the text is "estou resolvida a pôr em prática este meu propósito, por isso que sou assim ousada no que lhe diz respeito" (*Amigo*, III, p. 15).

[10]The use of "senhor" instead of "amigo" should, I think, be viewed here as an expression of the girl's anger—she is distancing herself from the addressee, not showing him deference. At II 2 both B and V read "o mentiral". Nunes (XII) prints this, Lang (LXXXV) and Machado (526) emend to "o[u] mentir al". Cf. Nunes, *Amigo*, v. III, p. 18. At II 4, Michaëlis ("Zum liederbuch," pp. 528-529) suggests "senher"—which probably should be read.

[11]At II 1, Lang (LXXXVI) and Nunes (XIII) read "El me estava," Machado (527), "Eu m estava." Moura (whose reading is given by Machado) reads more or less with the manuscripts, "E hu m' estava." Cf. Baveca, B 1224=V 829, vv. 8-11: "Per boa fe, amiga, ben vus digo/ que, hu estava migu' en vós falando,/ esmoreceu e ben, assy andando,/ morrerá, se vus d'el doo non filha." (Text from Zilli, p. 99). The stanza makes much more sense if the first verse is read in this way as a subordinate temporal clause: "and while he was talking to me about you..." Manuel Rodrigues Lapa, *Miscelânea de lingua e literatura portuguêsa medieval* (Rio de Janeiro: Instituto Nacional do Livro, 1965), p. 20, note 2.

[12]In the Galego-Portuguese lyric a male speaker will ask a lady not to be upset because he loves her, but he will not warn her that she should confine herself to this minimum of receptivity.

[13]The phrases "do que fez" (II 2) and "do que foy" (II 3) seem specifically to avoid any mention of the incident—as though no reference to the indiscretion noted in no. 9 were needed.

[14]I use the word "softening" in a precise sense. In the terminology of Latin love poetry the girl had been "dura" and is now "mollis."

[15]In the summary immediately following the analysis of this text I shall be content to refer to this poem as "Other" (i.e. "Other Woman"), but its generic classification in the world of communication which we are observing must surely depend on the function of the utterance in the praxis of the drama. I shall therefore refer to this poem in later summaries and in the conclusion as belonging to the genre

Komos.

[16]Stanza VI (in my text) is missing in B and V. Its reconstruction—assuming it belongs in the text—is obvious: VI 1=IV 2; VI 2=VIII 1. I take "amigo" at I 1 and "amado" at II 1 to be vocatives, but cf. Michaëlis, "Zum liederbuch," p. 529; Nunes, *Amigo*, v. III, pp. 23-24.

[17]In the first verse of the poem the word "recado" was written and crossed out after "non chegou," (in B). Alfred Jeanroy, in *Les Origines*, p. 315, acknowledges that nos. 14-16 seem to belong together, but fails to see the connection between nos. 13 and 14, and between nos. 16 and 17, etc. For anyone who, like Jeanroy, accepts the existence of even so small a nucleus of *cantigas* (in this corpus) which belong together, the question becomes: where and according to what criteria do we decide that this sequence is bounded (on either side)?

[18]By "explicit renunciation" I mean the topos, "the renunciation proper." Cf. note 2 to the Introduction.

[19]At I.3 "liero" is the reading of V, "lieto" that of B. This line has caused considerable confusion, cf.: Lang, *Das Liederbuch*, p. 134; Carolina Michaëlis de Vasconcellos, "Zum Liederbuch," p.529; Nunes, *Cantigas d'amigo*, III, 25; Lapa, *Miscelânea*, p. 20; Machado, III, 190; Arthur T. Hatto, ed., *Eos, An Enquiry into the Theme of Lovers' Meetings and Partings at Dawn* (London, The Hague, Paris: Mouton, 1965), p. 306; Reckert, pp. 214-216.

[20]Cohen, pp 169-198.

[21]There are other possibilities. Lapa (*Miscelânea*, p. 20) suggests, "[s]eria mais simples considerá-lo um refrã antigo de *alba*, porventura de caráter litúrgico (a ida para a vigília?): *Alva é, vai liero!* = 'Já é dia, appressa-te!' " Machado (532) prints "Alua [h]e; uay liero!" Reckert, p. 215, would read "alva" as âlva (= "à alva") and with enjambment. Thus: "o amigo despediu-se da amiga ao amanhecer, deixando-a com saudades dele"; and "[a] cinta que lhe oferecera como prenda simbólica, e que ela agora veste todos os dias de manhã cedo." It seems possible that "liero" is equivalent here to the Latin "levis" meaning "light," "quick," and also "fickle."

[22]Cf. Hatto, pp. 305-306; Reckert, p. 215: "ele 'vai liero', partindo rápido e airoso para o grande mundo masculino de acção e da aventura. . ." etc. But cf. Tavani, "La poesia lirica," pp. 138-140, esp. p. 139: "Ancor più evidente risulta la abusività del termine [sc. *alba*], quando applicato a canzoni in cui compare la parola *alva* ma senza alcuna relazione con la conclusione di un convegno d'amore."

[23]I have not assigned the discourse of the mother (I 1, II 1) to any genre. Her presence is significant in the setting of the scene and therefore in the interpretation of the text, but her questions seem to function within the girl's discourse rather than autonomously.

[24]Cf. Reckert, 194-199; Antonio Gedeão, "'Ay flores, ay flores do verde pino," *Colóquio/Letras*, 26 (Julho 1975), pp. 45-53; Stegagno Picchio, *Lição*, pp. 32 note, 57; Dorothy Clotelle Clarke, "The Early 'seguidilla'," *Hispanic Review*, XII (1944), 211-222. I regret not having seen the interpretation of Aurelio Roncaglia (presented in Lisbon, May 1981 — I am not aware of its publication) mentioned in

Stegagno Picchio, *A lição do texto*, p. 32, note 6, and again in Gonçalves, *A lírica galego-portuguesa*, p. 61.

[25]Prof. Donald Pearce has suggested to me that this "second" speaker may be the girl herself, voicing her hope, and therefore also her loneliness, in antiphonal response to her own question.

[26]In both V and B "eno alto" is written next to II 3, instead of on its own line (II 4 in our text).

[27]This poem is treated by both Stephen Reckert and Helder Macedo in *Do Cancioneiro de Amigo*. Cf. esp. pp. 22-24, 51-60, 204-213.

[28]Ibid., 54-55, 57, 207-209.

[29]Macedo (ibid., p. 54-55) says that although the poem could be taken at the literal level as merely a brief description of a girl who goes to wash her clothes and becomes angry (taking the girl—"the white one"[?]— as the subject of "meteu-se," as does D'Heur, *Recherches* p. 538) when the wind carries them away, it actually describes "uma primeira experiência sexual." The symbolic overtones of this *cantiga* are obvious enough (including the phallic wind), and the text should be compared with the famous "levou- s' a louçana" of Pero Meogo, a poem which, like ours, is located in the exact center of its corpus. (Cf. the commentary in the edition of Azevedo Filho pp. 59-64, 90-91.) D'Heur, *Recherches*, p. 538, says "le vent symbolise, de manière assez transparente, l'ami." For the meaning of "alva" (= "dawn" or = "the white one" or both?), cf. Michaëlis, "Zum liederbuch," p. 529; Nunes, *Amigo*, III, p. 27; Tavani, "La poesia lirica," p. 139.

[30]Since the poem can be interpreted in several different ways and at different levels, it is simultaneously not only "pre- and post- consummation" but, as Macedo suggests (cf. the preceding note), the description of the encounter itself.

The attention which this poem has attracted shows one thing, at least: that the central *cantigas* (nos. 16 and 17) in this macro-poem of 32 have been perennial favorites. If, as has been said, a musical composition is judged on the strength of its climaxes, this composition has been successful.

[31]Both B and V give this text with the words "valha deus" attached to the first line, so that the tradition of printing a four line stanza in this poem is modern. Moreover, despite the popularity of this poem—which, along with nos. 13-17, has been often anthologized—the first verse is nearly always given as "amado e meu amigo," a reading which has no manuscript authority and which contradicts the parallelistic scheme in this poem: the first element of verses I 1 and I 3 is identical in the repetition at II 1 and II 3, respectively; the second element alone is changed. Likewise in the other stanzas. At III 3 and V 1 Machado (535) reads, with B, "bayorinho" and "bayorĩo," respectively. V gives "hayo rinho" and "bayorĩo." Moura (cited in Machado) and Braga give "bayoninho," Lang (XCIV) "baiosinho," Nunes (XXI) "baiozinho." See the note in Lang, *Das Liederbuch*, p. 135. The last stanza is reconstructed from the text itself (VI 1=IV 3, VI 3=V 3, with "amado" for "amigo" as in I 1 and II 1—at the end of the line, of course, and not in the first half).

[32]Cairns, *Generic Composition*, treats the travel genres extensively.    See

the Index of Genres and Examples, under "Epibaterion," "Propemptikon," "Prosphonetikon," "Syntaktikon."

[33]Ibid. See "schetliasmos" and "schetliastic" in the General Index.

[34]My reasoning here is based, of course, on inferences drawn from the sequence of situations in no. 17 and the present text. Reading no. 18 out of context, there would be no way to situate the departure at any given time of day (although, as Hatto points out in the appendix to *Eos*, pp. 775-776, the time of year may be indicated in the reference to the flowers of the pine.)

[35]There are, by my count, at least a dozen clear examples of Propemptika among the corpus of 500 or so (the number is disputed) *cantigas d'amigo*. Given the number of poems in which someone is either leaving or returning, all four travel genres are fairly well represented in the Galego-Portuguese lyric, although they seem not to have been accorded the status of genres. Cf. Silvio Pellegrini, "Sancio I o Alfonso X?" *Studj romanzi*, XXVI (1935), pp. 71-89; rpt. in *Studi*, pp. 78-93. Pellegrini offers a list of *cantigas* relevant to the problem, and makes some distinctions, but no one seems to have taken the question much further.

[36]In both V and B there is a second, fragmentary version of this *cantiga* among the *cantigas d'amor* of Dom Dinis (V 116, B 523 [bis]). The variants are given by Nunes (*Amigo*, III, 447-448) and Machado (III, 87-89). Some of these variants are obscene. For instance in B the eighth line of the text (=III 1) reads "e quãdo el vẽ hu vos fodes razõ"; and the eleventh line (= III 4-5) reads "olhos entẽdẽ q[ue] nõ pod el foder." In B "prazer" (I 5) appears at the beginning of I 6. The fact that this poem had already been copied once—and by the same copyist—may or may not bear on the fact that it is numbered "570" although the same number had been assigned to the preceding poem. Pellegrini (*Studi*, pp. 165-166) cites the dislocation of this text as proof that the manuscripts cannot possibly present the texts "secondo l'ordine in cui furono composti o pubblicati." What the dislocation shows, I think—assuming that the corruptions in the text found among the *cantigas d'amor* are due to faulty or facetious transmission and not to the existence of two versions by Dom Dinis himself—is that the komastic discourse of the male can be recognized by its thematic structure (sequence of functions). It seems probable that someone inserted the poem among the *cantigas d'amor* because it seemed so much like a male wooing-speech. It is, though with a substitute speaker. Given the dislocation of this poem, it is especially significant that our no. 21, in which the male voice is heard first, was not transferred to the *cantigas d'amor* .

[37]At I 3 B reads "e com osara," with an upward stroke curving to the left over the "o" in "osara," indicating "ou," as at 22.9, "põco," with a horizontal stroke over the first "o," stands for "pouco." "Ousar" is spelled with "ou" at II 2 and III 3. In the first verse of the refram "n[õ]" is required by the sense. At I 5 B gives "n9" (= "nos"), at II 5 and III 5, "u9" (= "vos"). Since "n" and "u" are easily confused, it seems possible that the reading was in fact "nõ," and not "non" or "nom" when the error was made, and that the "õ" was mistaken for "9" (= "os"). Neither "vos" nor "nos" would make much sense here, except as a playful conceit—and either reading

would be awkward ("it's a long time since he's come to see us [or 'you'], oh me and my eyes and my good looks!"). All the modern editors accept the change, though of course they differ in the treatment of the nasal.

[38] Yet one more variant of the topos referred to— depending on the precise context—as "boy's intention to return" (no. 2), "boy's promise to send a message or return" (no. 5), "assurance that boy will return" (no. 16), "boy's promise to return" (no. 27).

[39]B and V both give the last two words of I 3 in reversed order. The rhyme requires that they be switched and all editors accept this change. In the first line of the refram B and V both read "E aredes." Lang (XCVII) prints "E avede." Nunes follows Lang in the *Crestomatia Arcaica*, 5th ed. [1st ed., 1907], (Lisboa: Livraria Clássica Editora, 1959), p. 268, but offers "Faredes" (as does Braga) in *Cantigas d'amigo*, II, 25, and is followed in this by Machado (537). Moura (cited by Machado) gives "E avedes." With the indicative (whether "avedes" or "faredes") the line may be read as a question. The parallelism ("fazer...farey...fazēd...") favors some form of "fazer," and it is probable that the initial "F" was misread as an "E." At II 4, V gives "possy fazer," which is doubtless correct, esp. in view of the parallels at I 3 ("fazer hi") and III 4 ("hi faça"). At II 5 and III 5, B and V have an inverted "c" (= con) with a double squiggle (see Carolina Michaëlis de Vasconcellos, ed. *Cancioneiro da Ajuda* (Halle a.S.: Max Niemeyer, 1904), II, p. 166). At III 3, V has "perdon" which is probably to be preferred as well, but since I am introducing as few changes as possible into the text of B, I have let "pardon" stand.

[40]Thus at the 6/8 point in the first "strophe" of the macro-poem and again at the 6/8 point in the overall series. As has been noted (Introduction, note 7), several scholars have pointed out that this poem "should" be considered a *cantiga d'amor* according to the criterion given in the *poetica* in B. Since the text occurs in a privileged position and functions perfectly in the sequence of events and genres, I believe that its proper place is obvious. It does not matter particularly whether it is called "d'amigo" or "d'amor." One would think, however, that given the transgression of the "rule" offered by the "poetica," someone would have transferred the poem (like no. 19) to the *cantigas d'amor*. Since this did not happen it seems likely that it was obvious that the text belongs where it is.

[41]And as such can be compared with the six Komoi broken down in Appendix 1, whose sequences of functions are given in the chart at the beginning of the first chapter. Cf. Cairns, *Generic Composition*, pp. 158-176, and the included Komoi in no. 23 and in Lang CXXVI, vv. 15-18: "Disse-m'el: Senhor, creede/ que a vossa fremosura/ mi faz gram mal sem mesura,/ porem de mi vos doede." All five topoi of the Komos are referred to in these four brief (eight syllable) verses, leading one to believe that the "essence" of any genre (that is, the principal topoi and the typical sequence of functions, including the cadential function) may perhaps best be discerned by the analysis of included examples of that genre. Thus the famous *pastorela* of D. Johan d'Avoin (V 278, B 676) contains both an included Renunciation ("nunca molher crea per amigo/ poys ss o meu foy e non falou migo"

vv. 9-10) and, in the corresponding place in the second (of two) stanzas, an included Invitation ("deus ora vehess o meu amigo/ e averia gram prazer migo" vv. 19-20 [the readings are mine]). These verses of Avoin should be compared, for example, with nos. 13 and 27 in our corpus. For the tendency of the Portuguese *pastorela* to include the female discourse, see esp. Luciana Stegagno Picchio, "Filtri d'oggi."

[42]In the analysis of topoi, I have separated "boy's absence" from "boy's delay in returning," even though the distinction is impossible to maintain in the analysis of the sequence of functions in this text (e.g., "e par deus por que o nõ vei aqui" is already about his delay, and so his suspected infidelity, even though it seems merely to refer to his absence. The distinction between "absence" and "delay in returning" should, nevertheless be maintained, theoretically. In many texts in the Galego-Portuguese lyric the absence of the beloved is neutral—is not a prelude to an accusation of infidelity or perjury, much less to a renunciation—while in many others it is a prelude to a discourse of expectation (understood in this study to belong to the genre called "Invitation"). Thus in no. 16, the question, "Oh, God, where is he?" would be neutral, if considered out of context, yet in the context—of the *cantiga*, let alone that of the sequence of genres— is all too clear. For that reason, the *refram* of no. 16 is a perfect example of a polyvalent or ambiguous topos, a pivot chord by means of which the modulation of a sequence of functions may be suggested in one stanza, actualized in another, and concluded, now without irony, in another.

[43]At I 1, the text of B looks to be "mandar" (rather than "vi andar"), but "vi," though often written as two separate letters, is sometimes written together by our copyist in such a way as to render the two letters nearly indistinguishable from an "m." The reading of V is clearly "vi andar." For information on the copyists, see Anna Ferrari, "Formazione e struttura del Canzoniere Portoghese della Biblioteca Nazionale di Lisbona (Cod. 10991: Colocci-Brancuti)." *Arquivos do Centro Cultural Português*, XIV (1979), 27-142. At II 1, Lang (XCIX) has "trist' e", followed by Nunes (XXVI) and Machado (539). Compare 3.4, 12.10, 30.13. Michaëlis, "Zum Liederbuch," pp. 528, 530. At II 3, Monaci (p. 431) suggests "perdud' a"—printed by Lang and Nunes. In the manuscripts II 4 is divided: "vyu/ disse mh assy," and the last three words are given their own line. Braga, Lang, Nunes and Machado read "sofr' e a" at III 3.

[44]In the analysis of topoi in this text I have subdivided the topos of suffering to point out the amount of topical detail—all of which gives the effect of a parody. The parodic model is obviously the Komos (Cf. Ovid's famous "palleat omnis amans," etc., at *Ars Amatoria*, I, 729). Cf. note 41, above.

[45]In B this text has two numbers assigned to it: "575," written next to the first line of the first stanza; and "576," written next to the first line of the second stanza, which begins on the next page of the manuscript. Moreover, the first stanza, which is at the bottom of the right hand column of f. 128r° is followed by the rubric, "El Rey don denis," with the "R" and "y" of "Rey" extended—the former traced several inches to the right and beneath the words, the latter looping about to the left: in short, the most elaborate of the three presentations of the name of the King in his

"*cancioneiro*" (*d'amigo* and *d'amor*).

At the beginning of the *cantigas d'amor* (before B 497) and at the beginning of the *cantigas d'amigo* (before B 553) the name of Dom Dinis is given a more reserved treatment. I find it very odd that the Dinis' name should come here in an elaborate form in the middle of a *cantiga*. The *Tavola Colocciana* (ed. E. Gonçalves) presents the name of Dom Dinis three times, as follows: "497 El Rey dom Denis," "553 Dom Denis Rey di Portogal," "575 El Rey dom Denis." The next entry, of "El Rey don Alffonso" is given the number of 607, and in fact no. 606 is the last of the *cantigas* ascribed to Dom Dinis in B (though the attribution is disputed by Tavani, *Poesia del Duecento*).

I consider it of the utmost relevance that the *cancioneiro* of Dom Dinis (I am referring only to the love poetry) may—according to the evidence of the *Tavola* (a document whose place in the manuscript tradition is disputed)—once have contained, at the end of the collection, and therefore among the *cantigas d'amigo*, a group of 32 poems (numbered 575-606 in the manuscript in which they were contained). Since the numbering of Dom Dinis' *cancioneiro* is disturbed in the *cantigas d'amor* (cf. the table given in Pellegrini, *Studi*, pp. 175-178 and the discussion in Gonçalves, *Tavola*, p. 19) in such a way as to make space for *twenty* extra texts, and since twenty *cantigas d'amigo* follow the set of 32 which I am studying here, I would like to suggest that these 32 are the 32 indicated in the *Tavola*. For the relation between the *Tavola* and B, a subject of much discussion in recent years, see: Tavani, "La tradizione manoscritta della lirica galego-portoghese," *Cultura Neolatina*, XXVII (1967), 41-94, rpt. in *Poesia del Duecento*; Luís Filipe Lindley Cintra, *Cancioneiro português da Biblioteca Vaticana (Cód. 4803). Reprodução facsimilada*. (Lisboa: Centro de Estudos Filológicos, Instituto de Alta Cultura, 1973), pp. 13-14; Jean-Marie D'Heur, "Sur la tradition manuscrite des Chansonniers galiciens-portugais. Contribution à la Bibliographie générale et au Corpus des Troubadours," *Arquivos do Centro Cultural Português*, VIII (1974), 3-43; Tavani, "A proposito della tradizione manoscritta della lirica galego-portoghese," *Medioevo Romanzo*, VI (1979), 372-418; Gonçalves, "Tavola;" Anna Ferrari, "Formazione e struttura," pp. 27-142, especially pp. 75-80. The elaborate rubric in B after the first stanza of no. 24, must, I think, have been placed there mechanically, according to a table which referred to the numeration of another manuscript. Whether that manuscript contained the extra 20 *cantigas d'amigo* is impossible to say, but the numbering in the *Tavola* and the presence of the rubric in B at a position precisely 32 numbers from the end of Dinis' corpus (of love poetry) both point to the existence of a set of 32 *cantigas d'amigo* which has been displaced forwards *within* the Dionysian *cancioneiro*. Thus—and this is the hypothesis—when the 20 *cantigas d'amigo* (those which follow our 32) were inserted, the numbering of the *cancioneiro* of Dinis was changed to allow for inclusion of the extra 20 *cantigas* without perturbation of the final number ("606") assigned to the corpus of Dinis. If Tavani is right about that text (B 605-606 = V 208), it may have been inserted because, with all the disturbances in the copying, the *cancioneiro* of Dinis ended one number too soon,—ie. there had been an overcompensation for the inclusion of the 20 *cantigas*.

The division of verses between the two speaking personae in this text is given by Braga and Machado (540) as it is given here, but Lang (C) and Nunes (XXVII) divide the verses in what seems an incomprehensible way. Machado (v. III, pp. 206-209) surveys the problem of speaker alternation (cf. Micaëlis, "Zum liederbuch," pp. 529-530; Oskar Nobiling, "Zur Interpretation des Dionysischen Liederbuchs," *Zeitschrift für Romanische Philologie*, XXVII (1903), pp. 190-191). I confess I find it strange that the speaker pattern should ever have been the subject of confusion among such scholars. The girl's discourse is introduced each time by the word "amigo" and is confined each time to the first verse of the stanza, plus the first verse of the *fiinda*. At I 2, II 2, III 2, and IV 2, the boy responds, using the word "senhor" in the first verse of each of his responses. I see no problem whatever there.

The reading and interpretation of II 7 does, however, seem problematic. Both manuscripts read "euos," which seems clearly to be taken as "e vos." I believe that either "é vós" or "é vos" would make sense here: "since it's you," or "since it's for you;" and there would be little difference between them. I take "hũa vez ia" to be elliptical. I 7 and III 7 both contain references to the speaker's imminent exile: "poys me sẽ vos vir," and "eu sẽ vos de moirer ey;" and in the last line of the *fiinda*, "mato mi" is an indirect reference to the speaker's exile—he will be killing himself by his departure. I think, then, that the first half of II 7, "mays poys e vos" belongs to the "service" topos, and the latter half, "hũa vez ia," to the topos of "exile." At III 2, V reads "qrrads". Nunes (following Braga) prints "querrá Deus", Lang offers "queirades". Cf. Michaëlis, "Zum liederbuch," p. 530. The colon at IV 2 is in B.

[46]Cairns, *Generic Composition*, where the subject is treated extensively (see "schetliasmos" and "schetliastic" in the "General Index," p. 320). Cf. the analysis of no. 18, above.

[47]At III 4, the "s" in "mays" is crossed out in B.

[48]I have not here assigned the boy's discourse (*fiinda*, 1-2) to a genre, for a reason similar to that given in note 23, above (p. 111), with regard to no. 15. The boy's discourse does belong, however, to the topos of service (he is only too glad to serve her by remaining), and in that sense could be considered to belong to the thematics of the komos—although he delivers nothing approaching a wooing speech. He is being wooed, and this is precisely the point.

[49]In the sixth verse in each stanza B reads "per iuras;" V, "periuras." Braga and Lang follow V, Nunes and Machado follow B, which, I think, offers the better reading. Cf. the irony in Catullus (64.143): "nunc iam nulla viro iuranti femina credat."

[50]The *ate-fiinda* technique, by which the syntax is sustained uninterrupted from the first word to the last, is found, within this set of 32 texts, only here and in no. 32—that is, in the poems in first and last position in the final group of four (Michaëlis, "Zum liederbuch," p. 528, would include no. 10, but there is no inter-strophic enjambment in no. 10). At II 3, the reading is problematic. Despite the reading of V (n9...deu9), Braga and Lang (CV) have "nos ... nos," and Nunes

(XXXII) follows suit. Machado (545) reads "uos ... uos." At III 3, B and V both give "amiga," which seems clearly an error (cf. "amigo" at I 1,5; II 5; III 5). At III 2, where B has "nena," and V, "uena," Lang (CV) reads "e-na," Nunes (XXXII) "ena," and Braga and Machado (545) "e en a." Could "nen" not function here much like the Provençal "ni," as an emphatic, non-negative coordinating conjunction?

[51]At III 1, it might be better to read, with the editors, "madr' e". This poem is almost certainly an imitation of Avoin (V 277, B 675) where the *refram* is "cada que migo quiserdes falar,/ falade migu' e pês a quen pesar" (Nunes, *Amigo*, CIX).

[52]Cf. Lanciani, *Il canzoniere di Fernan Velho*, p. 116, who cites Nunes XLVI (but not no. 31) as well as two *cantigas* of Avoin (Nunes CIII, CV). Fully half of Avoin's *cantigas d'amigo* are Renunciations, three of them quite explicit (see note 2 to the Introduction). Cf. also Baveca's "Amigu, entendo que non ouvestes" (Nunes CCCCXLII) and the comment in Zilli, *Johan Baveca*, p. 116.

[53]The shift is admittedly abrupt, but this abruptness may be ascribed to an ironic intent on the part of the poet. The girl who just was swearing that she would defy her mother at any cost to see her friend is now singing another tune. Thus no. 31 retroactively colors no. 30.

[54]See, above all, Silvio Pellegrini, "Appunti su una canzone di re Dionigi e sulla fortuna di 'Occasio' nella penisola iberica," *Archivum Romanicum*, XVI (1933), pp. 439-459, rpt. in _____ *Studi*, pp. 141-160, and the bibliography cited there. Pellegrini would read, with Michäelis, "ocajon," and argues his case most compellingly. It is out of deference to the manuscript, and not in defiance of Pellegrini's erudition and logic, that I print "caiõ." Could the word have been intended here as tri-syllabic (coming as it does from "casio-n-")—to be pronounced "ca-[j]i-õ"?

[55]At II 2, Moura, Braga, Lang and Nunes read "sol," which is the reading of V, and, as far as I can tell from the facsimile editions (Machado, Cintra), also of B. Machado, however, gives the reading of B as "s' el" and prints this in his text.

## Notes to Chapter Three

[1]The girl's most intimate confessions are to the mother, in the last group of each half. It is to the mother that she turns when she is dying of love in nos. 14 and 15, and to the mother that she addresses the final renunciation of the boy in no. 32. The affair is discussed at length with the friend in the first half, and, to a lesser extent, in the second. The boy speaks at the beginning of the sixth group (just as his message had arrived in the sixth poem of the first quarter) and by the second poem of the seventh group he has uttered his last words in the series. The girl's world thus extends outward from mother to friend to boy and then retreats back from boy to friend to mother. The boy is more important to her than the friend (once the boy speaks his complex discourse at no. 24, the friend has all but disappeared and figures

thereafter only as addressee in no. 28), but the mother is a final refuge from the cruelty of the amorous realm. The climactic moments in the series — whether we define these in terms of the complexity of the microsequence, the variety of genres, or the variation in speaker and addressee (including the use of dialogs) — come at the end of the first half and the very beginning of the second (nos. 15-17), and then in the series of encounters with the boy starting at no. 21 and lasting until the end of the set.

[2]The mother's discourse in no. 15, and the boy's in no. 26, both consisting of a mere two verses, do not figure here, for the reasons given in notes 23 and 48 to the second chapter. It should be remembered, however, that nos. 15 and 26 are dialogs. In the chart showing the distribution of genres in the second half of the series, the boy's discourse in no. 26 is referred to by the symbol "K" (=Komos).

[3]For the designation of no. 26 as I/K, see note 48, p. 117.

[4]The question of the Galego-Portuguese poem cycle has been discussed by Tavani in the *La poesia lirica*, pp. 58-61. See also the references given in note 11 to the Introduction (p. 105, above). My concern here is not the comparative study of these poem cycles, but rather the analysis of the corpus at hand, and my purpose has been to demonstrate, by a synchronic description, that it does contain such a "cycle". Although both Pellegrini and Tavani have rejected the possiblity, I trust that this description will at least have reopened the question.

[5]Tavani, *La poesia lirica*, pp. 58-59, 61.

[6]Margit Frenk Alatorre, *Las jarchas mozárabes y los comienzos de la lírica románica* (Mexico: El Colégio de México, 1975).

# Appendix 1

## The Breakdown of Six Komoi

Se eu podess ora meu coraçom

| | | |
|---|---|---|
| I. | 1 | Lady, if I could now force |
| | 2 | my heart to be able to tell you |
| | 3 | how much pain you make me suffer |
| | 4 | for you, I think, so help me God, |
| | 5 | that you would have pity on me. |
| | | |
| II. | 1 | For, Lady, though you treat me bad |
| | 2 | and never wanted to do me good, |
| | 3 | if you knew how much bad comes to me |
| | 4 | from you, I think, by almighty God, |
| | 5 | that you would have pity on me. |
| | | |
| III. | 1 | And though you bear me a great lack of love, |
| | 2 | if you knew how much bad I've borne for you, |
| | 3 | and how much pain since I've loved you, |
| | 4 | I think, in good faith, Lady, |
| | 5 | that you would have pity on me. |
| | | |
| IV. | 1 | And it would be bad, if it weren't that way. |

Lang XXI (100) Se eu podess' ora meu coraçom

**I**

| | | |
|---|---|---|
| 1) suffering | 3-4 | (quanta coita mi fazedes sofrer / por vós) |
| 2) request | 4-5 | (cuid' eu, assi Deus mi perdom, / que averiades doo de mi) |

**II**

| | | |
|---|---|---|
| 1) cruelty | 1-2 | (me fazedes mal / e mi nunca quizestes fazer bem) |
| 2) suffering | 3-4 | (quanto mal mi vem / por vós) |
| 3) request | 4-5 | (cuid' eu, par Deus que pód' e val, / que averiades doo de mi) |

III

| | | |
|---|---|---|
| 1) cruelty | 1 | (mh avedes gram desamor) |
| 2) suffering | 2-3 | (quanto mal levei / e quanta coita, des que vos amei) |
| 3) request | 4-5 | (cuid' eu, per bõa fe, senhor, / que averiades doo de mi) |

IV

1) suffering}
2) cruelty}          (E mal seria, se nom foss' assi)
3) request}


Que estranho que mh é, sehnor

|      |   |                                               |
|------|---|-----------------------------------------------|
| I.   | 1 | How strange it is for me, Lady,               |
|      | 2 | and what a great pain to endure,              |
|      | 3 | when I think about myself, to remember        |
|      | 4 | how much bad I have suffered                  |
|      | 5 | since that day I saw you,                     |
|      | 6 | and I have suffered all this bad              |
|      | 7 | for you and for your love.                    |
|      |   |                                               |
| II.  | 1 | For from that time, Lady,                     |
|      | 2 | that I saw you and heard you speak,           |
|      | 3 | I haven't lost sorrow and pain,               |
|      | 4 | nor could any bad be more,                    |
|      | 5 | and that's the way it's gone,                 |
|      | 6 | and I have suffered all this bad              |
|      | 7 | for you and for your love.                    |
|      |   |                                               |
| III. | 1 | And so, Lady, it would be                     |
|      | 2 | a great good of you to take                   |
|      | 3 | mercy on me who've sorrow without peer,       |
|      | 4 | and you know perfectly well                   |
|      | 5 | it's gone on and goes on in me,               |
|      | 6 | and I have suffered all this bad              |
|      | 7 | you and for your love.                        |

Lang XLV (125) Que estranho que mh é, senhor

I

| | | |
|---|---|---|
| 1) suffering | 1-4 | (Que estranho que mh é, senhor, <br> e que gram coita d'endurar, <br> quando cuid'em mi, de nembrar <br> de quanto mal fui sofredor) |
| 2) praise | 5 | (des aquel dia que vos vi) |
| 3) suffering | 6 | (e tod' este mal eu sofri) |
| 4) service | 7 | (por vós e polo voss' amor) |

II

| | | |
|---|---|---|
| 1) praise | 1-2 | (Ca des aquel tempo, senhor, / que vos vi e oi falar |
| 2) suffering | 3-6 | (nom perdi coitas e pesar, <br> nem mal nom podia maior, <br> e aquesto passou assi: <br> e tod' este mal sofri) |
| 3) service | 7 | (por vós e polo voss' amor) |

III

| | | |
|---|---|---|
| 1) request | 1-3 | (E porem seria, senhor, <br> gram bem de vos amercear <br> de mim) |
| 2) suffering | 3 | (que ei coita sem par) |
| 3) cruelty | 4-5 | (de qual vós sodes sabedor <br> que passou e passa per mi) |
| 4) suffering | 6 | (e tod' este mal sofri) |
| 5) service | 7 | (por vós e polo voss' amor) |

Pois ante vós estou aqui

| I. | 1 | Since I'm here before you, |
|---|---|---|
|    | 2 | Lady of my heart, |
|    | 3 | by God think it reasonable, |
|    | 4 | for all the bad I've suffered, |
|    | 5 | that you want to take pity on me, |
|    | 6 | or that you let me die. |

| II. | 1 | And since you know about the bad |
|---|---|---|
|    | 2 | that I've borne for so long, |
|    | 3 | think it now good, Lady, |
|    | 4 | by God, since I've gone through such bad, |
|    | 5 | that you want to take pity on me, |
|    | 6 | or that you let me die. |

| III. | 1 | And since I live in such pain |
|---|---|---|
|    | 2 | that I've lost sense and repose, |
|    | 3 | think it now good, |
|    | 4 | Lady, since my bad is so big, |
|    | 5 | that you want to take pity on me, |
|    | 6 | or at least that you want me to be well. |

Lang LXI (141) Pois ante vós estou aqui

I

| 1) service | 2 | (senhor d'este meu coraçom) |
|---|---|---|
| 2) request | 3,5 | (teede por razom // de vos querer de mi doer) |
| 3) suffering | 4 | (por quanto mal por vós sofri) |

II

| 1) suffering | 1-2 | (E pois do mal que eu levei / muit' a, vós sodes sabedor) |
|---|---|---|
| 2) request | 3,5 | (teede ja por bem, senhor // de vos querer de mi doer) |
| 3) suffering | 4 | (pois tanto mal passei) |

III

| 1) suffering | 1-3 | (E pois que viv' em coita tal / por que o dormir e o sem / perdi) |
|---|---|---|
| 2) request | 3-5 | (teede ja por bem, / senhor ... // de vos querer de mi doer) |

3) suffering     4     (pois tant' é o meu mal)


De mi valerdes seria, senhor

I.      1       Lady, it would be decorous for you
        2       to heal me for all I've served you,
        3       but since you don't like it that way,
        4       and I always have your worst bad,
        5       see if now it wouldn't be better,
        6           just as you like to let me die
        7           that you like to heal me.


II.     1       You wouldn't be making a mistake
        2       at all, for I know how to love you
        3       as well as I do, and since it pains you
        4       and I suffer the bad from which I'm dying,
        5       see now if it wouldn't be better,
        6           just as you like to let me die,
        7           that you like to heal me.


III.    1       There would be real utility in healing me
        2       for all I lose, and I'll tell you
        3       that means my body and God, and I never wronged you
        4       and I even like my pain, but now
        5       see if it's good, so please you,
        6           just as you like to let me die,
        7           that you like to heal me.


IV.     1       God darn me if in healing me
        2       you'd lose your good name
        3       since I love you so, and by God, who made you
        4       worth more than all the women in the world,
        5       see now if it's not reasonable,
        6           just as you like to let me die,
        7           that you like to heal me.


V.      1       And Lady, since yours is the power,
        2       by God, choose the better.

Lang LXIX (149) De mi valerdes seria, senhor

I

| | | |
|---|---|---|
| 1) request | 1-2 | (De mi valerdes seria, senhor, / mesura) |
| 2) service | 2 | (por quant' a que vós servi) |
| 3) cruelty | 3 | (mais pois vos praz de nom seer assi) |
| 4) suffering | 4 | (e do mal ei de vós sempr' o peior) |
| 5) request | 5,7 | (veed' ora se seria melhor // de vós prazer de mi querer valer) |
| 6) cruelty | 6 | (como vos praz de me leixar morrer) |

II

| | | |
|---|---|---|
| 1) request | 1-2 | (De mi valerdes, senhor, nulha rem / nom errades) |
| 2) service | 2-3 | (pois vos sei tant' amar / como vos am') |
| 3) cruelty | 3 | (e pois vos é pesar) |
| 4) suffering | 4 | (e sofr' eu mal de que moir') |
| 5) request | 5,7 | (veed' agora se seria bem // de vós prazer de mi querer valer) |
| 6) cruelty | 6 | (como vos praz de me leixar morrer) |

III

| | | |
|---|---|---|
| 1) request | 1 | (De mi valerdes era mui mester) |
| 2) service | 2-3 | (por que perço quanto vos *eu* direi, o corp' e Deus, e nunca vos errei) |
| 3) cruelty | 4 | (e pero praz-vos do meu mal) |
| 4) suffering | 4 | (meu mal) |
| 5) request | 4-5,7 | (mais er / veede se é bem, se vós prouguer,// de vós prazer de mi querer valer) |
| 6) cruelty | 6 | (como vos praz de me leixar morrer) |

IV

| | | |
|---|---|---|
| 1) request | 1-2 | (De mi valerdes, Deus nom mi perdom, / se vós perdedes) |
| 2) praise | 2 | (do vosso bom prez) |
| 3) service | 3 | (pois vós tant' am') |
| 4) request | 3,5,7 | (e por Deus ... // ve*e*d' agora se *nom* é razom // de vos prazer de mi querer valer) |
| 5) praise | 3-4 | (e por Deus que vos fez / valer mais de quantas no mundo som) |
| 6) cruelty | 6 | (como vos praz de me leixar morrer) |

V

| 1) request | 1-2 | (E pois, senhor, em vós é o poder, |
|---|---|---|
| | | par Deus, quered' o melhor escolher) |

## Senhor, em tam grave dia

| I. | 1 | Lady, I saw you on such a grave day |
|---|---|---|
| | 2 | that it couldn't be worse, |
| | 3 | and by Santa Maria, |
| | 4 | who made you so compassionate, |
| | 5 | have pity on me someday, |
| | 6 | lovely Lady. |

| II. | 1 | Since you're so sensible |
|---|---|---|
| | 2 | and good and wise, |
| | 3 | and God made you a face |
| | 4 | that he made for no other, |
| | 5 | have pity on me someday, |
| | 6 | lovely Lady. |

| III. | 1 | And by God, Lady, be |
|---|---|---|
| | 2 | sensible in view of the great bounty |
| | 3 | that He gave you, and look |
| | 4 | what a wretched life I lead |
| | 5 | and have a little pity |
| | 6 | on me, lovely Lady. |

## Lang LXXIII (153) Senhor, em tam grave dia

I

| 1) suffering | 1-3 | (em tam grave dia / vos vi que nom poderia / mais) |
|---|---|---|
| 2) praise | 3-4 | (e por Santa Maria, / que vos fex tam mesurada) |
| 3) request | 5-6 | (doede-vos algum dia / de mi) |
| 4) praise | .6 | (senhor bem talhada) |

II

| 1) praise | 1-4 | (Pois sempre a em vós mesura |
|---|---|---|
|  |  | e todo bem e cordura, |
|  |  | que Deus fez em vós feitura |
|  |  | qual nom fez em molher nada) |
| 2) request | 5-6 | (doede-vos por mesura / de mim) |
| 3) praise | 6 | (senhor bem talhada) |

III

| 1) request | 1-3 | (E por Deus, senhor, tomade |
|---|---|---|
|  |  | mesura por gram bonade |
|  |  | que vós el deu) |
| 2) suffering | 3-4 | (e catade / qual vida vivo coitada) |
| 3) request | 5-6 | (e algum doo tomade / de mi) |
| 4) praise | 6 | (senhor bem talhada) |

Senhor, eu vivo coitada

| I. | 1 | Lady, I live in sorrow |
|---|---|---|
|  | 2 | since I haven't seen you, |
|  | 3 | but since you want it this way, |
|  | 4 | by God, lovely Lady, |
|  | 5 | you should want to have pity on me, |
|  | 6 | or let me go die. |

| II. | 1 | By God, my beautiful Lady, |
|---|---|---|
|  | 2 | you have such power |
|  | 3 | over me that my bad and my good |
|  | 4 | is all in you, and so |
|  | 5 | you should want to have pity on me, |
|  | 6 | or let me go die. |

| III. | 1 | And for you I live such a life |
|---|---|---|
|  | 2 | that now these eyes of mine |
|  | 3 | never sleep, my Lady, and by God, |
|  | 4 | who made you so replete with good, |

|     |     |                              |
| --- | --- | ---------------------------- |
|     | 5   | you should want to have pity on me, |
|     | 6   | or let me go die.            |
|     |     |                              |
| IV  | 1   | For, Lady, all my pleasure   |
|     | 2   | is whatever you want to do.  |

Lang LXXV (155) Senhor, eu vivo coitada

I

| 1) suffering | 1-2 | (Senhor, eu vivo coitada / vida des quando vós nom vi) |
| ------------ | --- | ------------------------------------------------------ |
| 2) cruelty   | 3   | (mais pois vós queredes assi)                          |
| 3) praise    | 4   | (senhor bem talhada)                                   |
| 4) request   | 4-5 | (por Deus ... / querede-vos de mim doer)               |
| 5) suffering | 6   | (ou ar leixade m'ir morrer)                            |

II

| 1) praise   | 1   | (mha senhor fremosa)                                                   |
| ----------- | --- | ---------------------------------------------------------------------- |
| 2) service  | 2-4 | (vós sodes tam poderosa / de mim que meu mal e meu bem / em vós é todo) |
| 3) request  | 5-6 | (e porem / querede-vos de mim doer)                                    |
| 4) suffering | 6  | (ou ar leixade m'ir morrer)                                            |

III

| 1) suffering | 1-3 | (Eu vivo por vós tal vida / que nunca estes olhos meus /dormem) |
| ------------ | --- | -------------------------------------------------------------- |
| 2) praise    | 3-4 | (e por Deus / que vos fez de bem comprida)                     |
| 3) request   | 5   | (querede-vos de mim doer)                                      |
| 4) suffering | 6   | (ou ar leixade m'ir morrer)                                    |

IV

| 1) service | 1-2 | (Ca, senhor, todo m'é prazer / quant' i vós quizerdes fazer) |
| ---------- | --- | ------------------------------------------------------------ |

# Appendix 2

## Rhymes in Poem-Final Position

I will limit myself here to analyzing a single pattern: the pattern of rhymes in final position at the end of each of the 32 texts. I do not believe that I will be chastized for taking as premise the principle that the final position in any musical structure is privileged. In fact, there is a rather high degree of organization in the set of final rhyme sounds evidenced in these 32 texts. The final rhyme sounds can be divided into four classes: 1. tonic vowel (a,e,o) + r; 2. feminine rhymes; 3. tonic vowel alone (i,e,ey); 4. nasalised tonic vowel alone (ẽ). Since the set of 32 texts divides into eight groups of four, we may observe what sound is final in the last text in each group of four. These sounds are: **igo, er, er, e,er, ey,er,ẽ**. The last position in the first group of four is the only last position in a group of four which does not contain a masculine rhyme with **e**. The set-up also divides into four groups of eight. If we observe the sound which is final in the last text in each group of eight we see that this sequence: **er, e, ey, ẽ**; is even more exact. Moreover, **e, ey**, and ẽ occur in this set in final position only in these texts (16, 24, 32), which are the texts which mark the end of the half, the third quarter and the entire series, respectively. **ey**, the only dipthong in final position, marks the end of the third quarter, and ẽ, the only nazalized tonic vowel in final rhyme, marks the end of the set. It would take an elaborate statistical analysis to show what the probabilities against this are, but we need only point out that in the remaining 20 cantigas—those which do not form part of this set of 32—the final rhyme is "ẽ" three times. A look at the chart will show how carefully these rhyme sounds have been organized. (A feminine rhymes occurs in last position only in the first group of four, hence never in the last position in a group of eight. The feminine rhymes are distributed—three in the first eight, and two in each of the other three groups of eight. The tonic + r rhyme occurs three times in the first group of four in each of the first three groups of eight. The "or" rhyme occurs in the second half of the second and third groups of eight once, and no other "vowel + r" rhyme occurs along with it in those groups of four. The tonic vowel **i** begins the second group of eight, is penultimate—before **ey**—at the half and begins the last group of four.)

| | Tonic Vowel + R | Feminine Ending | Tonic Vowel | Nasalized Tonic Vowel | |
|---|---|---|---|---|---|
| 1 | AR | | | | 1 |
| 2 | AR | | | | 2 |
| 3 | AR | | | | 3 |
| 4 | | IGO | | | 4 |
| 5 | | IA | | | 5 |
| 6 | | EDES | | | 6 |
| 7 | AR | | | | 7 |
| 8 | ER | | | | 8 |
| 9 | | | I | | 9 |
| 10 | ER | | | | 10 |
| 11 | ER | | | | 11 |
| 12 | ER | | | | 12 |
| 13 | | ANA | | | 13 |
| 14 | OR | | | | 14 |
| 15 | | ERO | | | 15 |
| 16 | | | E | | 16 |
| 17 | | ALVA | | | 17 |
| 18 | AR | | | | 18 |
| 19 | ER | | | | 19 |
| 20 | ER | | | | 20 |
| 21 | OR | | | | 21 |
| 22 | | ADA | | | 22 |
| 23 | | | I | | 23 |
| 24 | | | EY | | 24 |
| 25 | ER | | | | 25 |
| 26 | | ARDES | | | 26 |
| 27 | | IGO | | | 27 |
| 28 | ER | | | | 28 |
| 29 | | | I | | 29 |
| 30 | AR | | | | 30 |
| 31 | ER | | | | 31 |
| 32 | | | | Ẽ | 32 |

# Bibliography

Annicchiarico, Annamaria. "Per una lettura del canzoniere di Johan Vaasquiz de Talaveyra." *Annali dell' Istituto Universitario Orientale di Napoli—Sezione Romanza*, XVI (1974), 135-157.

Asensio, Eugenio. *Poética y realidad en el cancionero penisular de la Edad Media*. 2nd ed. Madrid: Gredos, 1970.

Azevedo Filho, Leodegário A. de, ed. *As cantigas de Pero Meogo*. Rio de Janeiro: Edições Gernasa, 1974.

Bell, Aubrey F.G. "The Hill Songs of Pero Moogo." *The Modern Language Review*, 17 (1922), 258-262.

_____, C. Bowra, William J. Entwistle. *Da poesia medieval portuguesa*. Trans. António Álvaro Dória. 2ª ed. ampliada. Lisboa: Edição da Revista 'Occidente,' 1947.

Beltrami, Pietro G. "Pero Viviaez: Poesie d'amigo e satiriche." *Studi Mediolatini e Volgari*, XXVI (1978-1979), 107-124.

Bertolucci Pizzorusso, Valeria. "Libri e canzonieri d'autore nel medioevo: Prospettive di ricerca." *Studi Mediolatini e Volgari*, XXX (1984), 91-116.

_____. "Note linguistiche e letterarie di Angelo Colocci in margine ai canzonieri portoghesi." *Atti del Convegno di Studi su Angelo Colocci (Jesi, 13-14 settembre, 1969)*. Città di Castello: n.p., 1972, 197-203.

_____. "Le poesie di Martin Soares." *Studi Mediolatini e Volgari*, X (1962), 9-160; rpt. *Le poesie di Martin Soares*. Bologna: Libreria Antiquaria Palmaverde, 1963.

_____. "Le postille metriche di Angelo Colocci ai canzonieri portoghesi." *Annali dell'Istituto Universitario Orientale di Napoli-Sezione Romanza*, VIII (1966), 13-30.

Boase, Roger. *The Origin and Meaning of Courtly Love. A Critical Study of European Scholarship*. Manchester: Manchester University Press; Totowa, New Jersey: Rowman and Littlefield, 1977.

Braga, Theóphilo, ed. *Cancioneiro portuguez da Vaticana. Edição crítica*. Lisboa: Imprensa Nacional, 1878.

Cairns, Francis. *Generic Composition in Greek and Roman Poetry*. Edinburgh: Edinburgh University Press, 1972.

_____. "Self-Imitation within a Generic Framework. Ovid *Amores* 2.9 and 3.11 and the *Renuntiatio Amoris*." In *Creative Imitation and Latin Literature*. Eds. David West & Tony Woodman. Cambridge: Cambridge University Press, 1979, pp. 121-141.

Carter, Henry H., ed. *Cancioneiro da Ajuda. A Diplomatic Edition*. New York: Modern Language Association; London: Oxford University Press, 1941.

Cintra, Luís F. Lindley, intro. *Cancioneiro da Biblioteca Nacional (Colocci-*

*Brancuti); Cód. 10991; Reprodução Facsimilada*. Lisboa: Imprensa Nacional-Casa da Moeda, 1982.

———, intro. *Cancioneiro português da Biblioteca Vaticana (Cód. 4803); Reprodução Facsimilada*. Lisboa: Centro de Estudos Filológicos, Instituto de Alta Cultura, 1973.

Clarke, Dorothy Clotelle. "The early 'seguidilla'." *Hispanic Review*, XII (1944), 211-222.

Cohen, Rip. "The 'Renuntiatio Amoris' in 'Canção X'." *Quaderni Portoghesi*, 7-8 (Primavera-Autunno 1980), 169-198.

Costa Pimpão, A[lvaro] J[úlio] da, ed. *Cantigas d'el rei D. Dinis*. Lisboa: Livraria Clássica Editora, 1942.

Cotarelo Valledor, A[rmando], ed. *Cancionero de Payo Gómez Chariño*. Madrid: Librería General de Victoriano Suárez, 1934.

Cropp, Glynnis M. *Le Vocabulaire courtois des troubadours de l'époque classique*. Genève: Droz, 1975.

Cunha, Celso Ferreira da, ed. *O cancioneiro de Joan Zorro*. Rio de Janeiro: Imprensa Nacional, 1949.

———. *O cancioneiro de Martin Codax*. Rio de Janeiro: n.p., 1956.

Davis, W. M. "Análise literária de uma cantiga de D. Dinis." *Luso-Brazilian Review*, I, 2 (1964), 51-62.

De Lollis, Cesare. "Cantigas de amor e de maldizer di Alfonso el Sabio re di Castiglia." *Studj di Filologia Romanza*, II (1887), 31-66.

———. "Dalle cantigas de amor a quelle de amigo." *Homenaje a Menéndez Pidal*. I. Madrid: 1925, 617-626.

Deyermond, Alan. "The Love Poetry of King Dinis." In *Florilegium Hispanicum. Medieval and Golden Age Studies presented to Dorothy Clotelle Clarke*. Ed. John S. Geary, Charles B. Faulhaher & Dwayne E. Carpenter. Madison, Wisc.: Hispanic Seminary of Medieval Studies, 1983, pp. 119-30.

D'Heur, Jean-Marie. "L' 'Art de Trouver' du Chansonnier Colocci-Brancuti. Édition et analyse." *Arquivos do Centro Cultural Português*, IX (1975), 321-398.

———. "Nomenclature des troubadours galiciens-portugais (XIIᵉ-XIVᵉ siècles). Table de concordance de leurs chansonniers, et liste des incipit de leurs compositions." *Arquivos do Centro Cultural Português*, VII (1973), 17-100.

———. *Recherches internes sur la lyrique amoureuse des troubadours galiciens-portugais (XIIᵉ-XIVᵉ siècles)*. Liège: Publications de la Faculté de Philosophie et Lettres de l'Université de Liège, 1975.

———. "Sur la tradition manuscrite des Chansonniers galiciens-portugais. Contribution à la Bibliographie générale et au Corpus des Troubadours." *Arquivos do Centro Cultural Português*, VIII (1974), 3-43.

———. *Troubadours d'oc et troubadours galiciens-portugais. Recherches sur quelques échanges dans la littérature de l'Europe au Moyen-Âge*. Paris: Fundação Calouste Gulbenkian- Centro Cultural Português, 1973.

Diez, Friedrich. *Ueber die erste portugiesische Kunst-und Hofpoesie.* Bonn: E. Weber, 1863.

Donati, Cesarina. "Pero Goterres, cavaliere e trovatore." *Studi francesi e portoghesi* 79. L'Aquila: Japadre Editore, 1979, pp. 67-92.

Dronke, Peter. *Medieval Latin and the Rise of the European Love-Lyric.* 2nd ed. Oxford: Clarendon Press, 1968.

Ferrari, Anna. "Formazione e struttura del Canzoniere Portoghese della Biblioteca Nazionale di Lisbona (Cod. 10991: Colocci-Brancuti)." *Arquivos do Centro Cultural Português,* XIV (1979), 27-142.

Finazzi-Agrò, Ettore, ed. *Il canzoniere di Johan Mendiz de Briteyros.* Romanica Vulgaria. Collezione di testi medievali romanzi diretta da Giuseppe Tavani, 2. L'Aquila: Japadre Editore, 1979.

———. "Le due cantigas di Roy Gomez de Briteyros." *Estudos Italianos em Portugal,* 38-39 (1975-1976), 183-206.

Frank, István. *Répertoire métrique de la poésie des troubadours.* Paris: Champion, 1953-1957.

Frenk Alatorre, Margit. *Las jarchas mozárabes y los comienzos de la lírica románica.* México: El Colegio de México, 1975.

———. "La lírica pretrovadoresca." In *Les genres lyriques.* Tome 1, Fascicule 2. *Grundriss der Romanischen Literaturen des Mittelalters,* II. Heidelberg: Universitätsverlag, 1979.

Gangutia Elícegui, Elvira. "Poesía griega 'de amigo' y poesía arábigo-española." *Emérita,* XL (1972), 329-396.

Gedeão, António. "Ay flores, ay flores do verde pino." *Colóquio/Letras,* 26 (Julho 1975), 45-53.

Gonçalves, Elsa, and Maria Ana Ramos. *A lírica galego-portuguesa.* Lisboa: Comunicação, 1983.

Gonçalves, Elsa. "La Tavola Colocciana: Autori Portughesi." *Arquivos do Centro Cultural Português,* X (1976), 387-448.

Hatto, Arthur T. *Eos. An Enquiry into the Theme of Lovers' Meetings and Partings at Dawn.* London - The Hague - Paris: Mouton, 1965.

Hernadi, Paul. *Beyond Genre: New Directions in Literary Classification.* Ithaca and London: Cornell University Press, 1972.

Hitchcock, Richard. *The Kharjas: A Critical Bibliography.* London: Grant & Cutler Ltd., 1977.

Huber, Joseph. *Altportugiesisches Elementarbuch.* Heidelberg: Carl Winter, 1933.

Indini, Maria Luisa, ed. *Bernal de Bonval. Poesie.* Biblioteca di Filologia Romanza diretta da Giuseppe E. Sansone, 32. Bari: Adriatica Editrice, 1978.

Jakobson, Roman. "A textura poética de Martim Codax." In *Do cancioneiro de amigo.* By Steven Reckert, Helder Macedo. 2nd. ed. Documenta Poética, 3. Lisboa: Assírio & Alvim, n.d. [1st ed. 1976], 35-47. [="Lettre à Haroldo de Campos sur la texture poétique de Martin Codex," in *Questions de poétique.* Paris: Seuil, 1973, pp. 293-298.]

Jauss, Hans Robert. "Theory of Genres and Medieval Literature." In *Toward an Aesthetic of Reception*. Trans. Timothy Bahti. Minneapolis: University of Minnesota Press, 1982. [Originally in *Grundriss der Romanischen Literaturen des Mittelalters*, VI. Heidelberg: Universitätsverlag, 1972].

Jeanroy, Alfred. *Les Origines de la poésie lyrique en France au moyen-âge*. [1889] 3rd ed. Paris: Librairie Ancienne Honoré Champion, 1925.

Jensen, Frede. *The Earliest Portuguese Lyrics*. Odense: Odense University Press, 1978.

Lanciani, Giulia, ed. *Il canzoniere di Fernan Velho*. Romanica Vulgaria - Collezione di testi medievali romanzi diretta da Giuseppe Tavani, 1. L'Aquila: Japadre Editore, 1977.

Lang, Henry R[oseman], ed. *Das Liederbuch des Königs Denis von Portugal*. Halle A.S.: Max Niemeyer, 1894; rpt. Hildesheim-New York: Georg Olms Verlag, 1972.

──── . "The Text of a Poem by King Denis of Portugal." *Hispanic Review*, 1 (1933), 1-23.

Lapa, Manuel Rodrigues. "Cajon ou ocajon? (A proposito do v. 12 do C. V. no. 186)." *Revista Lusitana*, XXVIII (1930), 297-298.

──── , ed. *Cantigas d'escarnho e de mal dizer dos cancioneiros medievais galego-portugueses*. 2nd. ed. Vigo: Editorial Galaxia, 1970.

────, *Lições de Literatura Portuguesa. Época Medieval*. 10th ed. Coimbra: Coimbra Editora, 1981.

──── . *Miscelânea de língua e literatura portuguêsa medieval*. Rio de Janeiro: Instituto Nacional do Livro, 1965.

──── , *Das origens da poesia lírica em Portugal na idade média*. Lisboa: ed. do autor, 1929.

Le Gentil, Pierre. *La poésie lyrique espagnole et portugaise à la fin du Moyen Âge*. 2 vols. Rennes: Plihon, 1949-1952.

Macchi, Giuliano. "Le poesie di Roy Martinz do Casal." *Cultura Neolatina*, XXVI (1966), 129-157.

Machado, Elza Paxeco e José Pedro Machado, eds. *Cancioneiro da Biblioteca Nacional (Colocci-Brancuti)*. 8 vols. Lisboa: Ed. da 'Revista de Portugal', 1949-1964.

Majorano, Matteo, ed. *Il canzoniere di Vasco Perez Pardal*. Bari: Adriatica Editrice, 1979.

Marroni, Giovanna. "Le poesie di Pedr'Amigo de Sevilha." *Annali dell'Istituto Universitario Orientale di Napoli-Sezione Romanza*, X (1968), 189-339.

Martínez Torner, E. *Lírica hispánica: relaciones entre lo popular y lo culto*. Madrid: Castalia, 1966.

Méndez Ferrín, X. L. *O cancioneiro de Pero Meogo*. Vigo: Galaxia, 1966.

Menéndez Pidal, Ramón. *Poesía juglaresca y orígenes de las literaturas románicas*. 6th. ed. Madrid: Instituto de Estudios Políticos, 1957.

———. "La primitiva lírica europea. Estado actual del problema." *Revista de Filología Española*, XLIII (1960), 279-354.

Mettmannn, Walter, ed. Afonso X, o Sabio. *Cantigas de Santa Maria.* 4 vols. Coimbra: Por ordem da Universidade, 1959-1972.

Michaëlis de Vasconcellos, Carolina, ed. *Cancioneiro da Ajuda.* 2 vols. Halle a.S.: Max Niemeyer, 1904.

———. "Glossário do *Cancioneiro da Ajuda.*" *Revista Lusitana*, XXIII (1920), 1-95.

———. "Zum Liederbuch des Königs Denis von Portugal." *Zeitschrift für Romanische Philologie*, XIX (1895), 513-541; 578-615.

Minervini, Vincenzo. *Le poesie di Ayras Carpancho.* Pubblicazioni della Sezione Romanza dell'Istituto Universitario Orientale, Testi, vol. VII. Napoli: Istituto Universitario Orientale, 1974.

Molteni, Enrico. *Il canzoniere portoghese Colocci-Brancuti, pubblicato nelle parti che completano il codice vaticano 4803.* Halle a.S: Max Niemeyer, 1880.

Monaci, Ernesto, ed. *Il canzoniere portoghese della Biblioteca Vaticana, messo a stampa.* Halle a.S.: Max Niemeyer, 1875.

Moura, Caetano Lopes de, ed. *Cancioneiro d'El Rei D. Diniz, pela primeira vez impresso sobre o manuscripto da Vaticana, com algumas notas illustrativas, e uma prefação historico-litteraria pelo Dr. Caetano Lopes de Moura.* Paris: J. P. Aillaud, 1847.

Nobiling, Oskar, ed.. "As cantigas de D. Joan Garcia de Guilhade, Trovador do seculo XIII." *Romanische Forschungen*, XXV (1908), 641-719.

———. "Zur Interpretation des Dionysischen Liederbuchs." *Zeitschrift für Romanische Philologie*, XXVII (1903), 186-192.

Nunes, José Joaquim. "Cajon ou ocajon? (A propósito do verso 12 do n° 186 do C.V.)" *Revista Lusitana*, XXVII (1929), 300-303.

———. "Cancioneiro de D. Dinis." *Miscelânea de estudos em honra de D. Carolina Michaëlis de Vasconcellos. Revista da Universidade de Coimbra*, XI (1933), 200-205.

———, ed. *Cantigas d'amor dos trovadores galego-portugueses.* Coimbra: Imprensa da Universidade, 1932; rpt. Lisboa: Centro do Livro Brasileiro, 1972.

———, ed. *Cantigas d'amigo dos trovadores galego-portugueses.* 3 vols. Coimbra: Imprensa da Universidade, 1926-1928; rpt. Lisboa: Centro do Livro Brasileiro, 1970.

———. *Compêndio de gramática histórica portuguesa (Fonética e morfologia).* 8th. ed. Lisboa: Livraria Clássica Editora, 1975.

———, ed. *Crestomatia arcaica.* 5th ed. Lisboa: Livraria Clássica Editora, 1959.

Pagani, Walter. "Il canzoniere di Estevan da Guarda." *Studi Mediolatini e Volgari*, XIX (1971), 51-179.

———. *Repertorio tematico della scuola poetica siciliana.* Biblioteca di Filologia Romanza diretta da Giuseppe E. Sansone, 12. Bari: Adriatica Editrice, 1968.

Panunzio, Saverio. "Per una lettura del canzoniere amoroso di Roy Queimado." *Studi Mediolatini e Volgari*, XIX (1971), 181-209.

—––, ed. *Pero da Ponte. Poesie.* Biblioteca di Filologia Romanza diretta da Giuseppe E. Sansone, 10. Bari: Adriatica Editrice, 1967.

Pellegrini, Silvio. "Appunti su una canzone di re Dionigi e sulla fortuna di 'Occasio' nella penisola iberica." *Archivum Romanicum,* XVI (1933), 439-459.

—––. "Il canzoniere di D. Lopo Liáns." *Annali dell'Istituto Universitario Orientale di Napoli-Sezione Romanza,* XI (1969), 155-192.

—––, Giovanna Marroni. *Nuovo repertorio bibliografico della prima lirica galego-portoghese.* Collezione di testi medievali romanzi diretta da Giuseppe Tavani, 3. L'Aquila: Japadre Editore, 1981.

—––. *Repertorio bibliografico della prima lirica portoghese.* Modena: Società Tipografica Modenese, 1939.

—––. *Studi su trove e trovatori della prima lirica ispano-portoghese.* 2ª ed. riveduta e aumentata. Biblioteca di Filologia Romanza diretta da Giuseppe E. Sansone, 3. Bari: Adriatica Editrice, 1959.

Pepió, Vicente Beltrán. "O vento lh'as levava: Don Denis y la tradición lírica peninsular," *Bulletin Hispanique,* LXXXVI, nos. 1-2 (Janvier-Juin 1984), pp. 5-25).

Plummer, John F., ed. *Vox Feminae: Studies in Medieval Woman's Song.* Kalamazoo, Michigan: Medieval Institute Publications, 1981.

Propp, Vladimir. *Morphology of the Folktale.* Trans. Laurence Scott. 2nd ed. 1968; rpt. Austin: University of Texas Press, 1979.

Radulet, Carmen M., ed. *Estevam Fernandez d'Elvas. Il Canzoniere.* Pubbl. dei seminari di Portoghese e Brasiliano della Facoltà di Lettere dell' Università di Roma e della Facoltà di Lingue dell' Università di Bari-Studi e Testi, 2. Bari: Adriatica Editrice, 1979.

Reali, Erilde. "Le 'cantigas' di Juyão Bolseyro." *Annali dell'Istituto Universitario Orientale di Napoli-Sezione Romanza,* VI, 2 (1964), 237-335.

—––. "Il Canzoniere di Pedro Eanes Solaz." *Annali dell'Istituto Universitario Orientale di Napoli-Sezione Romanza,* IV, 2 (1962), 167-195.

Reckert, Steven, Helder Macedo. *Do Cancioneiro de Amigo.* 2ª ed. Documenta Poética, 3. Lisboa: Assírio & Alvim, n.d. [1st ed. 1976].

Rodríguez, José Luis, ed. *El cancionero de Joan Airas de Santiago.* Santiago de Compostela: Universidad, 1980.

Roncaglia, Aurelio. "Di una tradizione lirica pretrovadoresca in lingua volgare." *Cultura Neolatina,* 11 (1951), 213-249.

Salomon, Louis B. *The Devil Take Her! A Study of the Rebellious Lover in English Poetry.* Philadelphia: University of Pennsylvania Press, 1931; rpt. New York: A.S. Barnes & Company, Inc., 1961.

Sansone, Giuseppe E. "Il canzoniere amoroso di Joan de Guilhade. Temi e tecniche delle 'cantigas d'amor' di Joan Garcia de Guilhade." *Annali dell'Istituto Universitario Orientale di Napoli-Sezione Romanza,* III (1961), 165-189.

Savona, Eugenio. *Repertorio tematico del dolce stil nuovo.* Biblioteca di Filologia Romanza diretta da Giuseppe E. Sansone, 23. Bari: Adriatica Editrice, 1973.

Scudieri Ruggieri, Jole. *Poesia cortese dei secoli XIV e XV nella penisola iberica.* Pubblicazioni dell'Istituto di Filologia Romanza di Roma-Testi e manuali, 43. Modena: Società Tipografica Modenese, 1956.

Sena, Jorge de. "Ensaio de uma tipologia literária." *Revista de Letras,* vol. I (1960), pp. 201-236; rpt. *Dialécticas Teóricas da Literatura.* Lisboa: Edições 70, 1977, pp. 23-106.

———. "Sistemas e correntes críticas." *O Tempo e o Modo,* 38-39 (Maio-Junho 1966), pp. 517-614; rpt. *Dialécticas Teóricas da Literatura.* Lisboa: Edições 70, 1977, pp. 109-167.

Spaggiari, Barbara. "Un esempio di struttura poetica medievale: Le *cantigas de amigo* di Martin Codax." *Arquivos do Centro Cultural Português,* XV (1980), 749-839.

Spina, Segismundo. *Do formalismo estético trovadoresco.* São Paulo: Faculdade de Filosofia Ciências e Letras, 1966.

Stegagno Picchio, Luciana. "Filtri d'oggi per testi medievali: 'Hũ papagay muy fremoso'." *Arquivos do Centro Cultural Português. Homenagem a Marcel Bataillon,* IX (1975), 3-41.

———. *A lição do texto. Filologia e literatura. I—Idade Média.* Lisboa: Edições 70, 1979.

———, ed. *Martin Moya. Le Poesie.* Officina Romanica, collana diretta da Aurelio Roncaglia, 11; Sezione di studi e testi portoghesi e brasiliani a cura di L. Stegagno Picchio, 6. Roma: Edizioni dell'Ateneo, 1968.

———. *La Méthode philologique.* 2 vols. Paris: Fundação Calouste Gulbenkian, Centro Cultural Português, 1982.

———. "Le poesie d'amore di Vidal, giudeo di Elvas." *Cultura Neolatina,* XXII (1962), 157-168.

———. "Sulla lirica galego-portoghese: un bilancio." *Études de Philologie Romane et d'Histoire Littéraire offertes á Jules Horrent.* Ed. Jean Marie D'Heur et Nicolleta Cherubini, Liège: 1980, pp. 333-350.

Tavani, Giuseppe, "Appunti sulla grafia e la pronuncia del portoghese medievale. I: Moirer-morrer." *Convivium* XXXI (1963), 214-216.

———. *Lourenço, Poesie e tenzoni.* Modena: Società Tipografica Editrice Modenese, 1964.

———. "Parallelismo e iterazione. Appunti in margine al criterio jakobsoniano di pertinenza." *Cultura Neolatina,* XXXIII (1973), 9-32.

———. *Poesia del Duecento nella Penisola Iberica. Problemi della lirica galego-portoghese.* Officina Romanica, collana diretta da Aurelio Roncaglia, 12; Sezione di studi e testi portoghesi e brasiliani a cura di Luciana Stegagno Picchio, 7. Roma: Edizioni dell'Ateneo, 1969.

———. "La poesia lirica galego-portoghese." In *Les Genres lyriques.* Tome 1, Fascicule 6. *Grundriss der Romanischen Literaturen des Mittelalters,* II. Heidelberg: Carl Winter, Universitätsverlag, 1980.

———, ed. *Le poesie di Ayras Nunez.* Milano: Ugo Merendi, 1964.

------ "A proposito della tradizione manoscritta della lirica galego-portoghese." *Medioevo Romanzo*, VI (1979), 372-418.

------ "A proposito di una 'nuova' edizione di Martin Codax." *Rassegna Iberica*, 10 (Mar., 1981), 15-22.

------ *Repertorio metrico della lirica galego-portoghese.* Officina Romanica, collana diretta da Aurelio Roncaglia, 7; Studi e testi portoghesi e brasiliani a cura di Luciana Stegagno Picchio, 5. Roma: Edizioni dell'Ateneo, 1967.

------ "Spunti narrativi e drammatici nel canzoniere di Joam Nunes Camanês." *Annali dell'Istituto Universitario Orientale di Napoli-Sezione Romanza*, II, 2 (1960), 47-70.

Todorov, Tzvetan. "The Origin of Genres." *New Literary History*, VIII, 1 (Autumn, 1976), 159-170.

Toriello, Fernanda, ed. *Fernand' Esquyo. Le poesie.* Pubbl. dei seminari di Portoghese e Brasiliano della Facoltà di Lettere dell'Università di Roma e della Facoltà di Lingue dell'Università di Bari-Studi e Testi, 1. Bari: Adriatica Editrice, 1976.

Williams, Edwin B. *From Latin to Portuguese.* 2nd ed. Philadelphia: University of Pennsylvania Press, 1962 [1st ed. 1938].

Zilli, Carmelo, ed. *Johan Baveca. Poesie.* Biblioteca di Filologia Romanza diretta da Giuseppe E. Sansone, 30. Bari: Adriatica Editrice, 1977.

Zumthor, Paul. *Essai de poétique médiévale.* Paris: Seuil, 1962.

Ysopete-Zaragoza, 1489

hic liber confectus est
Madisoni .mcmlxxxvii.